Welcome
into the
Light

FR. EMMANUEL GUKENA OKAMI

ISBN: 9798851155116

*****

IMPRIMATUR

Bishop Ayo Maria Atoyebi, OP
Bishop Emeritus of Ilorin Diocese, Nigeria

NIHIL OBSTAT

Very Rev. Fr. Stephen Audu
Ilorin Diocese, Nigeria.

*****

EDITOR

Lisa Timms
Our Lady of Peace Parish, Burnham, UK.

*****

Printed by:
Plush Prints & Paperworks
Benin City, Edo State
Nigeria

*This book is dedicated to the
members of the Commonwealth of
Catholic Christians
and
The Word of Life Ministry, UK.*

Welcome Into The Light

FOREWORD

In our desire to survive the world that we live in, we tend to focus on how busy we can be - from fulfilling duties to meeting expectations, often so busy being strong that we have no time to feel what is void inside us. When the emptiness from within looms, we are cornered and see everything in sight as dark and bleak and, unsurprisingly, arrive at the point of 'breakdown'. These are the times when we are confronted with questions that make us ponder the true essence of living and all the relationships we form along the way.

Welcome into the Light is Fr. Emmanuel Okami's latest book, conceived out of his burning passion and unwavering dedication to guiding, leading, and journeying with those who long to find light, and gain answers and helpful ways of living a meaningful and purposeful life.

I'm one of the many who have been blessed with the opportunity to work closely with Rev. Fr. Okami, from journeying with the youth to supporting adults preparing for sacraments. I am even more blessed to have read some of his many books, which have helped and inspired me in my life of faith.

This book is for anyone seeking to better understand the true purpose of life and for anyone longing to grow in a deeper relationship with the Trinity—the perfect epitome of the kind of relationship we must have. Topics in each chapter are ordered, containing scriptural texts, thought-provoking questions for reflection, and concrete ways and practical, helpful tasks to aid anyone who wishes to grow in faith and have a deeper relationship with our Lord Jesus Christ, the One True Light.

> *I am the light of the world. Whoever follows me will not walk in darkness but will have the light of life.*
>
> **John 8:12**

Maris Nicholson
Parishioner of St. Augustine RC Church,
Heelands, Milton Keynes. UK

★★★★★

AUTHOR'S NOTE

$\Rightarrow$ ✵ ✵ $\Leftarrow$

I am so delighted to present this book, *Welcome into the Light*. It has been a burden that the Lord laid in my heart. He has reminded me many times to put this book together and sent many people my way to whom I know this book will be of great help.

My aim for writing this book is to explain some aspects of the Christian life, to help those who seek knowledge of what the Christian life entails, and to have answers and to help those who have been drawn to the faith, so they grow in their relationship with Jesus.

People often come to the Church hungry but are lost in satisfying this hunger. People have questions they seek answers to but need help knowing where to get the correct answers. People want to go deeper, but they need direction.

I have met so many people who asked me, "Father, how do I grow in the faith? How do I experience God? What do I need to do to have a relationship with God that will be fulfilling and meaningful?"

Welcome into the Light is my response to these salient questions. This book covers topics such as: who am

I in Christ (identity), prayer, a relationship with the Holy Spirit, retreat as a means of spiritual growth, choosing a spiritual director, faith and the will of God, the place of suffering in the Christian life, fellowshipping with other believers, witnessing to the faith, participating in the life of the Church, etc.

I pray that those who read this book will better understand what it means to follow Jesus, so that they may be drawn more profoundly into their relationship with the Trinity. I pray that their spiritual journey will become more precise and their lives will become spiritually richer.

Yours in His vineyard,

Fr. Emmanuel G. Okami
A Priest of Ilorin Diocese, Nigeria,
On Mission in Northampton Diocese, UK.
Word of Life Ministry, UK.

★★★★★

REVIEWS

Welcome into the Light is a book authored by Rev. Fr Emmanuel Okami. This book will suit anyone seeking a more profound knowledge of God and His Word. Fr. Emmanuel has taken time to explain, through the guidance of the Holy Spirit, some fundamental aspects of our spiritual growth and relationship with God, and how to sustain this relationship. These important topics will also enhance our spiritual growth, as Fr. Emmanuel explains to us. Welcome into the Light is a must-read for anyone who seeks to maintain a relationship with God.

Sr. Evelyn Mario Okonta *EHJ*

★★★★★

People worldwide are preoccupied with many questions that bother them. However, there is hope in Him who offered to die for humanity - the Lord Jesus, whom God sent to die for the sin of humanity. Have you met Jesus?

Welcome into the Light provides insights and offers hope to anyone who seeks to develop a growing relationship with Jesus Christ. In this book, you will see what God wants for every one of us. Fr. Emmanuel Okami explains how knowing Jesus on a deeper, more personal level means seeing Him at work and sharing your heart with the Saviour. I recommend this book to anyone, especially those who question Christianity and desire more.

Catherine Waweru
Parishioner of Holy Family Church,
Wexham, Slough, UK.

★★★★★

Fr. Emmanuel Okami's book, *Welcome into the Light*, fully encapsulates the path we are all called to follow in Christ. By leading us on a Spirit-guided journey, chapter by chapter, we come to a deeper understanding of our true purpose and the destined life that we were created for. This book is another work of art added to Fr. Emmanuel's gallery, and I recommend it to anyone who yearns to learn more about Christ.

Natalya Bozkurt
Parishioner of St. Augustine RC Church,
Heelands, Milton Keynes, UK.

★★★★★

We recall the encounter of Philip with the Ethiopian Eunuch in the Acts of Apostles: *And the Spirit said to Philip, "Go over and join this chariot." So Philip ran to him, heard him reading Isaiah the Prophet, and asked, "Do you understand what you are reading?" And he said, "How can I unless someone guides me?" And he invited Philip to come up and sit with him* (Acts 8: 30-32). The Holy Spirit has done it again. Just as He invited Philip to teach the Ethiopian Eunuch, He has instructed Fr. Okami to teach new converts and remind members of the Body of Christ, the truth about God (the Trinity), the Church and how we can build a lasting relationship with Him. Indeed, *this is eternal life: they know you, the only true God, and Jesus Christ, whom you have sent* (John 17:3). This book, *Welcome into the Light*, is simply a guide to knowing Christ.

Happy reading!

Shalom!

Fr. Lawrence Adebisi

★★★★★

Welcome into the Light

FR. EMMANUEL GUKENA OKAMI

CONTENTS

⇒ 🗡 🗡 ⇐

★★★★★

CHAPTER 1

The Emptiness Within

¹ As a deer pants for flowing streams, so pants my soul for you, O God. ² My soul thirsts for God, for the living God. When shall I come and appear before God?

Psalm 42:1-2

I usually love to ask people to share their faith stories - how they came to have a relationship with the Lord. I particularly like to interview people who found faith later on in life. One of the common answers I have received from people is that many felt a painful emptiness in them that nothing they tried could fill. Many were seeking the truth and answers to some fundamental questions about life, their identity and purpose.

This emptiness and search for meaning and purpose are what has led many people to God, and having found God, their soul now feels at peace and satisfied.

My dear friend, there is a hunger in all of us; an emptiness in our souls that only God can fill. The problem is that many people try to satisfy this hunger and emptiness with other things, like pleasure, fame, money, sex, drugs, or alcohol. Many seek truth in self-religion, false philosophies, and pagan ideologies. This may appear to satisfy us for a short time, but in the long run, this leaves us more empty and unhappy. Many have even destroyed their lives through these fraudulent means and ways.

Here is the answer - **God has made us for Himself, and our souls can only find rest and truth in Him.**

God didn't create us to be wondering who we are and why we exist. He didn't create us as experiments. He created us for a purpose, and we cannot discover that purpose or fully become who we are created to be unless we have a relationship with Him, through Jesus, His Son.

When we come to know God, we find the answers that we are seeking, we find the truth about who we are and why we are here. We come out of darkness into light, we find joy and peace, we are adopted into the family of God. We receive forgiveness of our sins, we are made new, and we become heirs to the promises of eternal life. Our emptiness is filled with the joy of faith. When God becomes the centre of our lives, everything fits together, and we feel whole and complete.

★★★★★

CHAPTER 2

Jesus Is Calling You

As Jesus passed on from there, he saw a man called Matthew sitting at the tax booth, and he said to him, "Follow me." And he rose and followed him. ¹⁰ And as Jesus reclined at table in the house, behold, many tax collectors and sinners came and were reclining with Jesus and his disciples. ¹¹ And when the Pharisees saw this, they said to his disciples, "Why does your teacher eat with tax collectors and sinners?" ¹² But when he heard it, he said, "Those who are well have no need of a physician, but those who are sick. ¹³ Go and learn what this means: 'I desire mercy, and not sacrifice.' For I came not to call the righteous, but sinners."

Matthew 9:9-13

In the Gospel passage we have just read, Jesus called a tax collector to follow Him. A tax collector worked for the Romans against his people. Their salary came from the commission they got from squeezing every penny from their people. Being dubious was a necessary skill in this occupation, and tax collectors were generally unloved, rejected and despised by their people. A tax collector was often grouped with sinners.

Jesus called a tax collector to follow Him. He called Matthew from his dubious occupation, from a lifestyle of cheating people, and from an isolated life. He called him to follow, to be a disciple. Jesus saw something in Matthew that nobody else saw. There was a seed of greatness in Matthew - greatness that could only come to bloom when he was planted in the right field.

Jesus followed Matthew home, and Matthew called his friends, and they all experienced Christ. Christ doesn't despise or condemn anyone. He welcomes and forgives sinners, and He offers them a new life. He gives them hope, a fresh start, and a new opportunity to become great.

To the self-righteous people who despised others, Jesus made it clear that He has come to call the sinners, those unloved, those spiritually sick, those isolated, those who feel their lives are falling apart, those who are tired of how they are living and want a change.

Just as Jesus called Matthew, perhaps He is calling you. Like Matthew, you may be in the wrong relationship, occupation, association, in the wrong location, in the bondage of addiction. Maybe your life is empty or shallow. Maybe you feel you are too damaged and broken to be useful to anyone.

Jesus is calling you today - He loves you even when no one else does. He needs you. When we come to Him, He forgives our sins, and we become a new creation. Anyone who is in Christ Jesus becomes a new creation. Their record of sin is wiped out. They are forgiven, sanctified and justified (2 Corinthians 5:17).

When we surrender our lives to Him, He gives us a new experience of life, of love, of peace and of joy. He becomes our teacher, friend and Saviour. We have the hope of an eternal life of joy after death.

Jesus came to seek and save sinners like you and me. He came so that we can have abundant life (John 10:10).

Do you feel that Jesus is calling you like Matthew? Do you feel you need to repent of how you are living?

Do you think your life can be more meaningful and fruitful, productive and useful than this?

Do you feel an emptiness in you that cries to be filled?

Do you want a better life than you have right now?

Then decide to follow Jesus today. Do not delay. Like Matthew, you can say 'yes' and surrender your life to Jesus. Matthew eventually became an Apostle and an evangelist - he wrote the Gospel of Matthew.

Only in Jesus can we become who we are truly created to be. Only when we follow Jesus can we fully maximise our potential and reach our fullest capacity. If we follow anything or anyone that is not Jesus, we are on the wrong road to the wrong location. A life without Jesus is empty and incomplete.

Let us pray
(Prayer of Surrender)

Lord Jesus, just as you called Matthew and he followed, I want to follow you. I want to surrender my life to you. I confess I am a sinner, and you are the Saviour of people like me. Help me to dedicate my life to you and to find forgiveness, joy, peace and hope in you. Make me new and useful for your purpose. Amen.

Task

- Spend time alone, thanking the Lord for forgiveness and praying you may follow Him without returning to sin.

- Pray for your other friends, colleagues or people you know who need Christ in their lives. Pray that they, too, may hear the voice of the Lord in their hearts and follow Him.

- Read 1 Timothy 1:12-16. Here, St. Paul shares with us how God saved him from being a persecutor of Christians and a blasphemer and placed him on the road to becoming an Apostle.

> *[12] I thank Christ Jesus our Lord, who has given me strength, that he considered me trustworthy, appointing me to his service. [13] Even though I was once a blasphemer and a persecutor and a violent man, I was shown mercy because I acted in ignorance and unbelief. [14] The grace of our Lord was poured out on me abundantly, along with the faith and love in Christ Jesus.*
> *[15] Here is a trustworthy saying that deserves full acceptance: Christ Jesus came into the world to save sinners—of whom I am the worst. [16] But for that very reason I*

was shown mercy so that in me, the worst of sinners, Christ Jesus might display his immense patience as an example for those who would believe in him and receive eternal life.

▪ Read about the life of St. Ignatius of Loyola.

Peace be with you. As you have decided to follow Christ, He welcomes you to the family of His people.

CHAPTER 3

Responding to the Call to Follow Jesus

Jesus Calls His First Disciples

⁶Jesus walked beside the Sea of Galilee and saw Simon and his brother Andrew casting a net into the lake, for they were fishermen. ¹⁷ "Come, follow me," Jesus said, "and I will send you out to fish for people." ¹⁸ At once, they left their nets and followed him. ¹⁹ When he had gone a little farther, he saw James, son of Zebedee and his brother John in a boat, preparing their nets. ²⁰ Without delay, he called them, and they left their father, Zebedee, in the boat with the hired men and followed him.

Mark 1:16-20

The Bible tells stories of how Jesus called the twelve disciples, and many others, to follow Him. For instance, in the text above, from the Gospel of Mark, we read how Jesus called His first four disciples to follow Him. Jesus called Peter and told him that He would make him a fisher of people. He also called the others who were fishermen. They left everything and followed Him.

In the same way that Jesus called these four disciples and the others, He continues to call us today.

What is He calling us to and for?

I. He is calling us to a relationship of love. He calls us to know Him, to know His love for us and respond by loving Him in return.

II. He calls us to know ourselves. He reveals who we are to us and the essence of our existence. He calls us to where we can become who God has called us to become. In Matthew 9:9-13, we have the account of the call of Matthew. He called him from being a tax collector to becoming an evangelist. In the text above, He called the disciples from being fishermen to something bigger - to becoming an instrument of transforming the world.

III. He calls us to transform and give us a new identity. When He calls us, He calls us to come as we are, but He makes us new. He works daily in us for our transformation.

Many people are afraid to respond to the call of Jesus because they feel that it will diminish their lives and they will become so spiritual, dull, dry, and boring, but that's not true. He calls us to a better, fuller and richer life. He calls us to freedom, fruitfulness, and peace.

IV. He calls us to become a blessing in the world. In Matthew 5:13-16, He says that we are the world's light and the earth's salt. We are created to be a blessing, a solution, and a remedy in the world.

V. He calls us to learn from Him, to become like Him and to make Him known to others as the way to salvation, the truth that liberates and the life that is full, beautiful, incomparable, and eternal.

Whenever Jesus calls us, we must leave some things behind to follow Him. In the case of these disciples, they left behind their nets, occupation, familiar environment etc., and they followed Him.

Jesus doesn't often call us to leave our families or jobs to full-time ministry, but when He calls us, He calls us to prioritise Him above everything in our lives because He is worth more than everything. He calls us to bring everything to Him - our time, family, kids, jobs, family, future.

He calls us to dissociate ourselves from the false gods in our lives and the wrong things we subscribe to for peace, security, and pleasure. He calls us to come out of a life of sin. He calls us out of the slavery of addiction, from our uncontrollable quest for sexual satisfaction, our idolisation of money. He calls us out of inappropriate relationships and associations. He calls us from every wrong thing we have become a slave to. He calls us to follow Him and allow Him to make us new.

He is worth giving everything up for.

Jesus calls us in different ways. He calls some through the blessings He bestows upon them. He calls others through the tragedies of their lives. He calls many through their emptiness and searches for truth and meaning. He calls some people at their lowest moments, when they need someone to turn to. He calls many through the testimony of others. He calls people by speaking to their hearts. He calls people through their brokenness, disappointment, sicknesses, pain, grief, and frustration. Many have been called through visions and revelations etc.

Jesus calls all of us to follow Him but in different ways. Let us heed His call and follow because no one ever follows Jesus and regrets it. True life begins when we decide to follow the Lord.

CHAPTER 4

Faith in the Person and Work of Jesus

⁶Jesus answered, "I am the way, truth, and life. No one comes to the Father except through me.

John 14:6

God created every one of us to know Him, love Him, serve Him, and be happy with Him in this life and the next (Penny Catechism, art 1). However, through the sins of Adam and Eve, our first parents, and our sins, we have separated from God.

Jesus, the Son of God, took our sins upon Himself. He suffered and died on the cross to pay the price for our sins. He did this purely out of love and mercy. He did this to reconcile us back to the Father. He died and rose as proof that all He said was true and that His sacrifice had been accepted. The Bible bears witness to this, verifiable as a good history.

God bore witness to Jesus that He is the chosen One through whom we can obtain mercy, restoration, grace, forgiveness, new life, peace, adoption, the fullness of life and hope of eternal life. He is the way, the truth, and the life; no one can come to the Father except through Him (John 14:6).

We are invited to believe in Him and accept what He has done for us, to make a decision to follow Him and to open our hearts to Him.

The Bible tells us in John 1:12-13:

> *[12] To all who did receive him, who believed in his name, he gave the right to become children of God, [13] who were born, not of blood nor the will of the flesh nor the will of man, but of God.*

It is through Jesus that we can come to know the Father. St. Paul tells us in Colossians 1:15 that Jesus is the image of the unseen God. Jesus Himself tells us that no one has seen the Father except the Son, who has come to make Him known (John 1:18).

Through Jesus, we can call God our Father, and we come to understand the love and mercy of God. Through Him, we have access to the Father and can know Him and relate with Him.

Having believed in Jesus, He also calls us to follow Him and to grow in our relationship with Him.

CHAPTER 5

Who are You in Christ?

Once you had no identity as a people; now you are God's people. Once you received no mercy; now you have received God's mercy."

1 Peter 2:10

L et us reflect on our identity in Christ Jesus. Many people have crises of identity. Many people believe the lies of the devil and the negative judgements of others about them.

It is one thing when mean people are bullying us, but it is another thing when the bully is inside of us, when something in us is telling us that we are worthless, not good enough, that we are condemned and hopeless. This is why St. Paul tells us to hold every thought captive and force them to obey the law of Christ (2 Corinthians 10:5).

We are not defined by who someone says we are or what any voice of condemnation within us is saying. We are who God says we are. Our identity is not based on what we do or have done but on what God has done for us. Knowing who we are in Christ gives us joy, meaning, and purpose. It is a good foundation for building our relationship with God and others.

Who am I in Christ?

I.   In Christ, you are loved.
The God of the entire universe loves you with faithful, everlasting and unshakeable love. (Read Colossians 3:12; John 3:16). The Lord delights in you and rejoices over you (Psalm 18:19; Zephaniah 3:17; Isaiah 62:4).

II. In Christ, you are forgiven.
In Christ, you obtain forgiveness for all your sins through His blood. All your past mistakes have been forgiven and blotted out. You are justified and redeemed (Ephesians 1:7; Psalm 103:12; Hebrews 8:12).

III. You are chosen.
You are not here by mistake - God chose you before the foundation of the world. He created you for a specific purpose (1 Peter 2:9; Ephesians 1:4; 2 Timothy 1:9).

IV. You are a new creation.
Christ gives you a new identity, a new life. The things you could be ashamed of are taken from you; every day is a new and fresh start. You have no old

labels; you are completely new in Christ (2 Corinthians 5:17; Romans 6:6).

V. You are not condemned.
There is no condemnation for you in Christ Jesus. You have been set free from eternal condemnation by the sacrifice of Jesus on the Cross. He paid your ransom and redeemed you (Romans 8:1).

VI. You are victorious.
In Christ, you are more than a conqueror; you are victorious. You are not to live with a victim mentality - you are not a victim. You are on God's team; you are on the winning side (Romans 8:37; Romans 8:28; 1 Corinthians 15:57).

VII.   You are God's handiwork.
God created you as you are. He doesn't create rubbish, so you are not rubbish or worthless. You are wonderfully and fearfully made by God (Psalm 139:14). Isaiah 64:8 says:

> *Yet you, LORD, are our Father. We are the clay; you are the potter; we are all the work of your hand.*

(Read Ephesians 2:10)

VIII.   You are a work in progress.
You may not be perfect, but you are a work in progress. God is still working on you and will never give up on you (Philippians 1:6).

IX. You are blessed and rich in Christ.

You have been blessed with all the spiritual blessings in the heavenly places. In Ephesians 1:3, we read:

> *Blessed be the God and Father of our Lord Jesus Christ, who has blessed us in Christ with every spiritual blessing in the heavenly places.*

We are heirs of God and coheirs with Christ (Romans 8:17).

X. You are adopted into the family of God.

You are a child of God - the saints and angels are your siblings, God the Father is your Father, Jesus is your Brother, the Holy Spirit lives in you, and Mary is your Mother. Imagine the dignity of being a child of God, an anointed member of the Royal family of God.

St. Paul says in Ephesians 2:19:

> *So, you are no longer strangers and aliens, but you are fellow citizens with the saints and members of the household of God...*

(Read John 1:12; 1 John 3:1-2).

XI. You are a member of Christ's body.

In 1 Corinthians 12:27, we read:

> *Now you are the body of Christ, and each one of you is a part of it.*

You are not a visitor in the Church or a second-class member. You are part of Christ's Holy Body.

XII.   You are the temple of the Holy Spirit.
The Spirit that lives in Christ lives in you. The Holy Spirit lives in you, and He in you is greater than the Spirit in the world (1 Corinthians 3:16, 6:19; 1 John 4:4).

XIII.   God has made you the world's light and the earth's salt.
You are to lighten up the world and to season it. You make the world a better place, to preserve it from corruption and to bring to it the sweetness of the kingdom of God (Matthew 5:13-16).

XIV.   You are a friend of Jesus.
John 15:14-15 says:

> *14 You are my friends if you do what I command. 15 I no longer call you servants because a servant does not know his master's business. Instead, I have called you friends, for everything I learned from my Father I have made known to you.*

XV.   In Christ, you are accepted.
Ephesians 1:6-7 says:

> *To the praise of the glory of His grace, by which He made us accepted in the Beloved. In Him, we have redemption through His blood, the forgiveness of sins, according to the riches of His grace.*

You are not rejected; God willingly accepts you because of Christ. In essence, the Father has AC-CEPTED us willingly, with approval, with value, with esteem and with delight, not because we have merited His approval, but because His Beloved paid the price in full for our approval.

In conclusion, can you see how special you are in Christ Jesus? No wonder the Bible says you are the apple of God's eye.

> *Thus, the Lord of hosts says, "After glory, He has sent me against the nations which plunder you, for he who touches you touches the apple of His eye.*
>
> Zechariah 2:8

Let us no longer think of ourselves as worthless and purposeless. Let us rebuke every voice deceiving us into believing we do not belong. Let us embrace and believe everything God says and see ourselves as God sees us. Let us agree with God and accept ourselves as He accepts us. Then we can live as God intends and fulfil our glorious destiny.

I AM WHO GOD SAYS I AM.

★★★★★

CHAPTER 6

Faith and the Will of God

… for we walk by faith, not by sight.
2 Corinthians 5:7

The Bible teaches us in many places that our God is omnipotent and that He can do all things. He is not just omnipotent; He is also a loving Father. Hence, we can approach Him for our needs with faith and confidence, and we are assured that He will hear and answer us.

Jesus tells us in Mark 11:23-24:

> *"Truly, I tell you, if anyone says to this mountain, 'Go, throw yourself into the sea,' and does not doubt in their heart but believes that what they say will happen, it will be done for them. Therefore, whatever you ask for in prayer, believe that you have received it, and it will be yours.*

The issue here is that many people approach God with faith - they pray fervently for a particular intention, it could be for the recovery of a dear one, for healing for themselves, for a reversal of a situation, for a favour from someone, to get a job, to receive a positive result from an interview or examination, for conversion of a family member, for an end to a trial or temptation, etc., but they don't receive the answers they desire.

This is when many people get upset with God, and some even feel God has failed or disappointed them. Many then question His goodness, love, omnipotence, wisdom, and even His existence. This is why we must understand the relationship between faith and surrendering to God's will.

Faith in this context, is approaching God with our needs, with the confidence that He cares for us, loves us, and can do all things.

However, this is not all about faith. It is not enough to expect to receive what we ask for from an omnipotent God; our faith must be open to the will of God. Our faith must recognise the greater wisdom of God; our faith must recognise our limitations in understanding and reasoning; our faith must accept God's better plan for us.

This is why living faith is not believing that God will give us whatever we want, regardless of our request, but that His answer will always be the wisest answer to our ultimate good. Put differently, faith is not just the assurance that God will do what we ask but the ability to accept whatever answers God gives us, knowing that God has our best interests at heart (Jeremiah 29:11).

Many people know what the Word of God says in Matthew 7:7-8:

> *⁷ "Ask, and it will be given to you; seek and you will find; knock and the door will be opened to you. ⁸ For everyone who asks receives; the one who seeks finds; and to the one who knocks, the door will be opened.*

However, they do not realise that there are conditions attached. St. John helps us to understand this in 1 John 5:14 when He says:

> *¹⁴ This is our confidence in approaching God: if we ask anything according to his will, he hears us.*

Whatever we ask for must be according to the will of God. Whatever we need, we can take it to the Lord in prayer. However, the Lord will answer according to what is best for us. This may mean saying "No" to our request. He could say "Yes," but sometimes God says "Wait," and sometimes He gives us something different from what we ask for.

We must know that the response we get from God is motivated by His love for us. Even His "No" is for our good. This is why we need to be able to trust God with the outcome of our prayers and accept whatever He chooses for us.

A very practical and apt example is the prayer of Jesus in the garden of Gethsemane in Luke 22:42. Jesus thought about the suffering ahead of Him, and in His humanity, He trembled. He was about to take the sufferings of the whole world upon Himself. He was about to suffer the pain of temporal separation from the Father because of our sins. He was deeply troubled in His soul, and so He prayed, *Father, if you are willing, take this cup from me; yet not my will, but yours be done.* The Father heard His prayer. He sent an angel to strengthen Him, but the Father didn't remove the cup because it was necessary for our salvation.

The prayer of Jesus in this moment of agony should inform our prayers too. After stating our requests, needs and desires, our prayers should also end with: "However, not as I will, but your will be done."

This is what Jesus teaches us in the pattern of all prayers He gave us. He teaches us to pray that His will be done (Matthew 6:10). This tells us that our prayer must always align with His will. We must always submit to His will and recognise that His plans for us are superior to ours.

His word tells us in Isaiah 55:8-9:

> *For my thoughts are not your thoughts, neither are your ways my ways," declares the Lord. [9]"As the heavens are higher than the earth, so are my ways higher than your ways and my thoughts than your thoughts.*

I see in the request of the leper who approached Jesus for healing, an inspiring example of a powerful prayer. The leper said, *Lord, if you are willing, you can heal me and make me clean* (Matthew 8:2). This leper recognised the greatness of Jesus and His ability; however, he brought his request under His will... *"If you are willing…."*

Our desperation doesn't push God to act; He acts according to His love, plan, and wisdom. It is hard when we don't get what we desire. It even hurts, but then this is where a balanced faith is needed.

Some have even said that if, in the long run, it is God's will that prevails (Proverbs 19:21), why then should we pray? The simple answer is that we pray not to change God's will but to dispose ourselves to know and accept it. When we pray, we confess that we are aware of a particular need. Our prayers acknowledge that we need God to help us, that we are not independent and self-sufficient and that we don't have the means to provide what we need for ourselves.

Praying reminds us of the limitations of our humanity and the sovereignty of God. It honours God as our absolute helper and provider.

Let us therefore not get upset when God doesn't give us what we ask for or exactly what we ask for. Let us be assured that everything He does and everything He does or doesn't give is for our good. This is where we also need the Holy Spirit because the Holy Spirit helps us to pray according to the mind of God.

> *And he who searches our hearts knows the mind of the Spirit because the Spirit intercedes for God's people under the will of God.*
>
> Romans 8:27

The Holy Spirit helps us desire what God wills and helps us to surrender and accept what He gives. He purifies our will and aligns it with His will. This is the only way we can receive whatever God gives us, with gratitude, satisfaction, and a positive spirit.

★★★★★

CHAPTER 7

Understanding Suffering in Discipleship

I am now rejoicing in my sufferings for your sake, and in my flesh I am completing what is lacking in Christ's afflictions for the sake of his body, that is, the church.

Colossians 1:24

For Christians to build their faith on a solid foundation that can withstand the storm, they must properly understand the meaning and place of suffering in their spiritual journey.

Many people take offence at God and abandon their faith when they face serious crises, when they enter into the season of the storm, when they are confronted with the cross. Unfortunately, many preachers today are misleading people by not giving them a proper understanding of suffering in discipleship. Many people have a wrong understanding and believe that following Jesus protects them against life's crosses, storms, toils, and disappointments.

In this chapter, I just want to reflect on the place of suffering in the life of a believer and what should be our right disposition towards this. Having the right disposition is possible if we have the right understanding.

Let me begin by saying that everyone who exists, by our existence, must deal with one form of suffering or another. Whether we believe in God or not, as long as we exist, we live in a world where suffering is part of its organ and substance.

There are different kinds of sufferings in this world. In an article titled, 'Fourteen kinds of suffering', published on realfaith.com (2023), Mark Driscoll talks about fourteen kinds of suffering. Drawing inspiration from this, I will talk about twelve types of suffering, and I will divide these into natural and divine suffering.

Natural or General suffering

I. *Adamic suffering:*
We all face this suffering because we are part of the human race, and we are born into a fallen world. It is a suffering that we share in because we are implicated in Adam.

II. Demonic suffering:

These are sufferings caused to a person by evil spirits who are agents of the devil at work in the world.

III. Empathetic suffering:

This is when we suffer with the people we love.

IV. Punishment suffering:

This is when we suffer for an offence committed.

V. Consequential suffering:

This is the suffering that comes from our foolish decisions or wrong choices.

These five kinds of suffering are natural and general; everyone participates in them by being human and existing. I will now talk about seven kinds of divine suffering that have spiritual value.

I. Disciplinary suffering:

This is when God chastens us, just as a father chastises a child. This suffering is to train us in righteousness and make us mature and grow in our relationship with God (Hebrews 12:6).

II. Testimonial suffering:

This is when God uses our lives and experiences of suffering to strengthen others and evangelise. It is when He uses our lives as an example of faith, patience, courage, and perseverance to others. Good examples of this are Job and Joseph, the son of Jacob.

III. Preventive or providential suffering:
God sometimes allows us to suffer certain things to prevent us from greater suffering or evil. We may suffer a failed relationship or a disappointment, to prevent us from greater suffering or problems.

IV. Vicarious suffering:
This is when we suffer because of our faith and our association with Christ.

V. Atonement or purifying suffering:
Sometimes, God allows us to suffer things to atone for our past sins. God, in His providence, allows us to pay the temporal punishment due for our sin after its guilt has been removed through Confession. This purification is God's way of preparing us for heaven and giving us the grace to undergo our purgation here on earth, perfecting us and making us worthy of heaven.

VI. Examination suffering:
We go through these sufferings to test the depth, genuineness, and strength of our faith, our love for God, and how much we trust Him. God allows us to go through some suffering not to test

our faith and love but to allow us to prove our faith and love.

VII.   Mysterious suffering:
We do not know why we go through these sufferings, and we will never know why. Only God knows everything. This suffering doesn't make sense to us and is inexplicable, but it makes total sense to God. We shall understand why when we see the Lord face to face, where our knowledge will be perfected.

Even from our categorisation, we can draw some powerful lessons about suffering.

- Suffering is inevitable whether we are Christians or not.

- Rejecting the Lord and abandoning our faith because of suffering doesn't improve our lives. Rather, it makes us more miserable because our faith in the Lord gives us strength to deal with our sufferings and make them meaningful.

- For a child of God, there is purpose in every suffering. God will not allow us to go through anything if it is not for our good and His glory. There is no suffering that we go through that is purposeless. Some of our sufferings are used to discipline us or to make us an inspiration to others. Some are to atone for our past sins and to perfect us for heaven. Some sufferings are God's ways of schooling us to equip us for ministry and sometimes to prevent us from greater danger or evil. God may also permit some suffering to prove our faith and love.

- God will never allow us to endure any suffering that He hasn't prepared us for. He won't allow us to go through suffering without giving us the grace to bear it. He doesn't allow us to go through what is beyond our strength (1 Corinthians 10:13). The Bible says He gives to each of us according to our ability (Matthew 25:15).

- For those who believe in God and hold firmly to Him even in their sufferings, those who persevere in faithfulness to Him, their sufferings shall one day end. Our final home is heaven, where there is no suffering and pain. It is a place of perfect rest from our earthly labours (Revelation 21:1,4). It means all our sufferings are short-lived, and glory awaits us.

Suffering is temporal. In God's eternal plan, suffering is not included. St. Paul tells us in Romans 8:18:

> *Yet what we suffer now is nothing compared to the glory he will reveal to us later.*

Again, he says in 2 Corinthians 4:17-18:

> *[17] For our light and momentary sufferings are achieving eternal glory that far outweighs them all. [18] So we fix our eyes not on what is seen, but on what is unseen since what is seen is temporary, but what is unseen is eternal.*

In conclusion dear child of God, do not allow your suffering, pain, or cross to rob you of your faith or joy in the Spirit. Let nothing stop you from praising God and trusting Him. Your life is in His hands, and whatever He allows you to go through is because there is a purpose. With this understanding, let us face our sufferings with greater faith and a positive attitude.

I end with the Words of Jesus in John 16:33:

> *I have said these things to you, that you may have peace in me. In the world, you will have tribulation. But take heart; I have overcome the world.*

★★★★★

CHAPTER 8

Growing in the Lord

> *But grow in the grace and knowledge of our Lord and Savior Jesus Christ. To him be the glory both now and to the day of eternity. Amen.*
>
> **2 Peter 3:18**

After we have decided to respond to God's will for us to follow Jesus, the next step will be growing our relationship with Jesus. Just as physical growth and maturity are important to a living being, spiritual growth and maturity are also necessary for a Christian.

The question is: how do I grow in my relationship with Jesus?

There are many recommendations I will make here, and the other chapters in this book will develop on them.

We grow in our relationship with Jesus through the following:

- A life of prayer
- Daily study of God's Word
- Regular attendance at Mass and communal prayers of the Church.
- Fellowshipping with other Christians who are serious about their relationship with God and listening to testimonies of how God has moved in the lives of others.
- Finding time for retreat, reflection and meditation.
- Making regular Confession.
- Rendering service in the Church and contributing to the growth of the Church through our gifts, time, energy, and talents.
- Growing in knowledge of the faith and the truth of the Gospel through listening to good Christian messages and reading good spiritual books.
- Through spiritual direction and asking questions about areas in the Word of God, doctrine, and practices that we do not understand.
- By avoiding things that can come between God and us, especially sins.
- Making the Holy Spirit our friend. He is the one who orchestrates growth and maturity in the life of a believer.

Above all, a person who seeks to grow in the Lord must be willing to prioritise God in their schedules and to love Him with their hearts, minds, and souls.

★★★★★

CHAPTER 9

A Discourse on Prayer

Devote yourselves to prayer, keeping alert in it with thanksgiving.

Colossians 4:2

Let us reflect on the theme of prayer, focusing on the importance, place and power of prayer in the life of a Christian. Prayer is a wonderful privilege for every child of God. It is the ordinary way we communicate with God - we speak and we listen to Him as He speaks.

In the life of Christ, we have a great example of His commitment to prayers. As busy as He was, He was always slipping away from the crowd, sometimes long before dawn, to an isolated place to pray. In Luke 5:16, Jesus often withdrew to lonely places and prayed. This shows us an example of the importance and power of prayers. It is said that a prayerless Christian is a powerless Christian.

The Bible is also replete with examples of people

who prayed and experienced the power of God – Daniel, whose prayer blocked the mouths of lions; Elijah, who called down fire and caused the heavens to be shut so that there was no rain, and who then prayed again and there was rain; Moses who pleaded and the Lord showed mercy to His people. Joshua prayed and the moon stayed still till he conquered his enemies. David prayed, and the Lord turned the counsel of Ahithophel into foolishness. Jonah prayed and was delivered from the belly of the fish. The early Church prayed, and where they were was shaken. Paul and Barnabas prayed and praised God, and the prison gates were thrown open. The Church prayed for Peter, and God sent an angel to deliver him. These are just a few out of the many instances we are shown in the Bible.

St. John Damascene said that prayer raises the mind and heart of God. St. Thérèse of Lisieux describes prayer as a surge of the heart; it is a simple look towards heaven, a cry of recognition and love, embracing both trial and joy.

By prayer, one acknowledges God's power and goodness and one's need and dependence. Prayer presupposes faith in God and hopes in His goodness.

To grow in our relationship with God, we need to grow in our prayer life. Prayer is the soul of spirituality. Prayer must become part of our lives, something which we always do. Let us reflect on these points in prayer.

- *We should pray regularly:*

A regular prayer life is important for growth in the Lord. We must set time aside in the day to meet with God. It should be our time with God, and we must avoid all distractions, interruptions and disturbance and be fully and patiently present with the Lord - no calls, no mobile phones, and no allowing the mind to stray. Just be present with God, relax and have a conversation with Him.

Sometimes you may not feel like praying. Do not let your prayer life be directed by feeling - it is necessary.

- *Make prayer a priority:*

Prayer must always be our first response to anything. It must almost become instinctual, our natural first response. Do not postpone prayer or do it after you have done other interesting things and there is nothing else to do - no message to reply to, no one to chat with, so then you hastily chat with God. Prayer is the life of a believer. It is what strengthens our inner being and improves our re lationship with God. Prayer is never to be neglected, rushed or said mindlessly.

- *Pray constantly:*

St. Paul tells us to pray without ceasing (1 Thessalonians 5:17). We must, at all times, be in close fellowship with God. We must have an unbroken communion. Prayer must become part of all that we do. We should seize every opportunity to pray and pray in every circumstance (James 5:13). We must remain in God's presence, and the consciousness of God should be in whatever we are doing - driving, eating, bathing, cooking, washing, jogging, meeting, relaxing etc. At every opportunity, we can speak to God and listen to Him.

- *We must pray persistently:*

We must not just pray regularly but also persistently, without losing heart. This means that we must pray without giving up when we ask for something from God. It is not something we do only when in trouble but something that is part of who we are, part of our lives. Jesus uses the parable of a persistent widow in Luke 18:1-8 to teach us this great lesson. (Read also, Ephesians 6:18; Colossians 4:2; Philippians 4:6; 1 Thessalonians 5:17). In Luke 11:8-9, Jesus encourages us to ask God for what we need through prayers.

> [9] *"And I tell you, ask, and you will receive;
> seek, and you will find; knock and the
> door will be opened to you.* [10] *For everyone
> who asks, receives; and the one who seeks,
> finds; and the one who knocks, the door
> will be opened.*

- *A good prayer is not measured by length:*

Even though it is important to comfortably spend a
good length of time with the Lord in prayer, length
is not the measure of the strength of prayers.

- *Prayer should not be a mindless repetition of words*:

It is better to have minds without words than words
without our minds. One Hail Mary with proper
concentration is better than twenty decades mindlessly recited, which Jesus called 'babbling.' Meditating carefully on our words and intentionally
avoiding distraction is a good way to approach
prayer.

- *Fine words do not measure the efficacy of prayer.*

Sometimes we think someone who prays elo-
quently has prayed well. We think God is impressed
by fine words. Sometimes, when you ask someone
to pray, they say they don't know how to express
their words. Prayer is a communication of the heart,
and words from the heart are more acceptable than
words from the head. A beautifully expressed prayer

is not through being logical or poetic/rhythmic; it is expressing sincerely before God the true sentiments of our hearts.

- *Prayer is not meant to teach God what to do or make Him aware of what He is unaware of*:

We do not pray to teach or inform God. Rather, when we pray, we acknowledge/identify a need, confess that we depend on God to satisfy the need and ask to be disposed to receive what He is willing to give because His will is the best answer to prayers.

- *Prayer should proceed from and aim towards a deepening relationship:*

Prayer is meaningful when a relationship with God animates it. It is not just coming to ask the Supreme Being for what we need, and then, on receiving it, we go away. Prayer must proceed from, aim towards, and be fuelled by, a loving relationship with God. We pray to know God; the more we know Him, the better we pray.

Categories of prayers

- **Prayer of Thanksgiving:** Thanking God for what He has given, what He has done and what we trust Him to do.

- **Prayer of Adoration/ Praise:** To praise God for who He is - His greatness, power, love, kindness and justice. God is worthy of our praise, honour and worship. This is acknowledging that we are creatures standing before a Creator. This lauds God for His own sake and gives Him glory, quite beyond what He does, but simply because He is.

- **Prayer of Contrition:** A sincere regret and remorse for sin, resolution to avoid sin in the future, and conversion of the heart towards God, with hope in His mercy and trust in the help of His grace.

- **Prayer of Supplication:** This is a request to God asking Him to fulfil a need. By the prayer of petition, we acknowledge our dependence on God. This expression is not intended to instruct or direct God on what to do but to appeal to His goodness for the things we need. The appeal is necessary not because He is ignorant of our needs or sentiments but to give definite form to our desires, to express our dependence and help us appreciate our close personal relationship with Him. We can ask God for anything, no matter how great or small.

We can appeal to the following - the power in the name of Jesus, the power in His saving Blood, the merit of Christ's suffering, the power and promises of His saving Word, the intercession of the Mother of the Lord, the prayers of all Holy men and women.

- **Prayer of Intercession:** Prayer of intercession is also a form of prayer of petition. We ask for what we need for ourselves and others. Here we can pray for the world, the Church, civil and religious leaders, those who have asked us to pray for them, our relatives in the world or those who have gone before us. We pray for peace, persecuted Christians, conversion of sinners, troubled families, the sick, the elderly, children, parents, those who do not or no longer believe in God or have time for Him, souls in purgatory, etc. Prayer for others unites us more closely with Jesus, our greatest intercessor.

Types of prayers

Vocal: This is made by using some approved words, read or recited, e.g., the Lord's Prayer, Hail Mary, Prayer to our Guardian Angel, etc.

Mental: This is made without employing words or formulas of any kind. It is the mind's assent towards God. Here, the sentiments expressed are one's own.

In this form of prayer, one dialogues with God by meditating on His words and contemplating Him. There are two types of mental prayers: *Meditation and Contemplation.*

Meditation is a form of reflective prayer which engages thought, imagination, emotion and desire. Most meditative prayers use the Word of God or a spiritual reading, and the mind ruminates on them.

Contemplative prayer is a silent attentiveness, which looks at God by contemplating and adoring His attributes.

Different ways to pray

- Silence before God, just listening to Him and allowing Him to give us peace. This is most powerful when we are before the Blessed Sacrament.
- We can pray with the Bible, declaring the promises of God contained in His Word and listening as He speaks to us through His Word.
- We can say the prayers and devotions of the Church, like the Rosary, Divine Mercy chaplet, and the Rosary of our Lady of Sorrows. We can pray Novenas through the Saints' intercessions, as in many Catholic prayer booklets. We can pray the Divine Office (prayers to sanctify the hours of the day).

- We can pray alone or pray with others.
- The Mass is the highest form of Catholic prayer. It is participating in the redemptive mystery of Christ's death and Resurrection. It is the offering of Jesus as a sacrifice to the Father, to thank the Father for His Son, to obtain forgiveness and grace, and to obtain mercy for the living and the dead.

What prayer does

1. It makes us become like Jesus, who was a man of prayer.
2. Prayer strengthens our relationship with God.
3. God speaks to us in prayer to give answers, direction, and guidance.
4. Prayer strengthens us against temptation.
5. We receive revelations and insights through prayer.
6. Prayer gives us the grace to align our will with God's will.
7. It invites the Holy Spirit into our lives.
8. Prayer works miracles - healing, grace, peace, forgiveness and blessing.

Wrong understanding of prayer

- **Simple psychological activity:** Many people see prayer as a simple psychological activity, opium for relief. Prayer is a powerful communication with God, and it is very efficacious.

- **Ritual words:** Some people approach prayers as just ritual words and recite them mindlessly. Praying without meditating on our words or allowing wilful distractions is not a good prayer.

- **Prayer is to control or manipulate God:** Some people think prayer is unproductive and useless because they are disappointed at not being heard according to their own will. In prayer, we express our needs to God, but we surrender to His greater wisdom, perfect plans, and love for us. We do not seek to manipulate or coerce God but rather to submit to Him.

- **Prayer without work:** Some people try to pray without work, using prayers as a flight from work, from the world, and practical actions. Prayer and work go together. As we pray, we work; as we believe, we act.

- **Prayer as optional and facultative:** Some consider prayer unnecessary or the last resort when other options fail. Prayer is not optional or a last resort. It ought to be at the heart of our daily activities.

Prayer and the Christian life are inseparable. Through constant prayers, we communicate with God and invite Him into our lives and affairs. Through prayer, we sanctify our actions and invoke God's presence and power.

Difficulty in prayer

Distraction*: Many people complain of distraction in prayers.*

Sometimes we may not be able to avoid the distraction, but what is required is that we turn back to our heart or turn our heart back to our prayers. To avoid distractions, we need discipline and vigilance. We could even pray against it. We also need a settled mind to pray. For instance, praying immediately after watching a movie or engaging in a rough conversation may cause a serious distraction to the mind.

Dryness: *Sometimes, we experience dryness when praying; we feel disconnected.*

Should I still pray when I feel this way? Yes, prayer should be rooted in a decision to communicate with God and not in feeling. Even when we don't feel like praying, we must keep praying because it gives us spiritual energy and connects us to the source of our being. Even when we feel He is far away, He is always with us.

Anger: *Sometimes, we do not feel like praying because we are angry with God about a situation or unanswered prayers.*

Praying or praising God, even when we do not feel like it, is a great demonstration of faith (Job 13:15; Habakkuk 3:17-19).

Keys to efficacious prayers

- **Faith:** Believing that God is a loving Father who listens, hears, and answers prayers. Prayer is not an activity that merely brings psychological relief or a way of trying luck. To pray well, we must be convinced that we are talking to a Father who is living and loving, aware, able and available (Hebrews 11:6).

- **Forgiveness:** Unforgiveness can be an obstacle to prayer (Sirach 28:1-7)

- **Concentration/Attention:** We must pray before God's presence. It is better to have a heart without words than words without a heart.

- **Openness to God's will:** When we pray, we should be open to God's will. This stems from our recognition that He knows what is better for us and He won't deny us anything necessary for our wellbeing and salvation (1 John 5:14-15).

- **Rely on the merit of Christ:** When we come to God, we must not rely on our own good works or righteousness; we must rely on the merit of Christ and the power of His atoning sacrifice for us (Luke 18:10-14).

- **Perseverance**: We also need perseverance in prayer. Sometimes God tests our patience; He teaches us to wait. He prepares us for what we long for and He stretches and purifies our desires (Read Luke 18:1-8 and Hebrews 10:36).

- **Holiness of life**: The effort to live a good, holy and righteous life gives force and efficacy to our prayers. (Read James 5:16).

- **Openness to the Holy Spirit:** The Holy Spirit teaches us to pray according to the mind and will of God. He helps us to desire what God is willing to give us. He also enables us to find prayer delightful and joyful. He provides words and teaches us to pray in the Spirit and in truth (Romans 8:26-27).

Basic Catholic prayers

- ➢ The Sign of the Cross
- ➢ Our Father
- ➢ Hail Mary
- ➢ Apostles/Nicene creed
- ➢ Memorare
- ➢ Prayer before meals and after meals
- ➢ Prayer to our Guardian Angel
- ➢ Morning Offering
- ➢ Evening Prayer.
- ➢ Act of Contrition

➢ Prayers to the Holy Spirit.
➢ Come Holy Spirit.
➢ Divine Mercy Prayers
➢ The Angelus
➢ Prayer to St. Michael the Archangel

Principal prayers of the Church

- The Mass
- The Divine office
- The Rosary

Additional reading

The Psalms

The Psalms have always been an important part of Catholic liturgy. From earliest times until today, Christians viewed the Old Testament as prefiguring Christ. We heard the words of the Psalms on the lips of Jesus during His passion (Psalm 22, as per Matthew 27:46).

Along these lines, ancient monks and nuns in the Egyptian desert, heard Jesus' voice in all the Psalms. They believed that it was mainly King David who wrote the Psalms, but they also believed that the pre-existent Christ inspired David to do the writing (Psalm 110:1). For this reason, they prayed the whole Psalter daily. This tradition has grown and changed, but it remains faithful to the ancient practice. In Christian monasteries and many religious houses throughout the world, vowed men and women gather to pray the Psalms.

The Liturgy of the Hours is centred on chanting or recitation of the Psalms. Early Catholics also employed the Psalms widely in their prayers (Read Ephesians 5:19-20). Whenever we pray the Psalms, we unite our sentiment with that of Jesus and we pray with Him and allow Him to pray in us. He fulfils all the sentiments expressed in the Psalms.

We also have words from the Psalms that we can use for protection, safety, healing, thanksgiving, asking for forgiveness, petitioning, for praising God.

★★★★★

CHAPTER 10

Study Your Bible

This book of the law shall not depart out of your mouth; you shall meditate on it day and night, so that you may be careful to act in accordance with all that is written in it. For then you shall make your way prosperous, and then you shall be successful.

Joshua 1:8

One of the ways we can grow in our Christian life is through the daily study of God's Word. Many people have a wrong understanding of the Bible. Some think it is obsolete, fictional and of little or no relevance. Some think it is a collection of outdated stories designed to interest and entertain.

This is not true. The Bible is timeless and eternally new, life-giving and relevant. In Psalm 119:160, the Psalmist says, *All your words are true; all your righteous laws are eternal.*

We read in Isaiah 40:8:

> *The grass withers, and the flowers fall, but the word of our God endures forever.*

The Bible is a very powerful book - it is the Word of God in human language and written under the inspiration of the Holy Spirit. St. Paul tells Timothy about the inspiration of the Word of God.

> [16] *All Scripture is God-breathed (inspired) and is useful for teaching, rebuking, correcting and training in righteousness,* [17] *so that the servant of God may be thoroughly equipped for every good work.*
>
> 2 Timothy 3:16-17

It is a book of revelation - that is, it contains God's self-disclosure. This means that through reading the Bible, we come to a deeper understanding of who God is - His will, nature, and ways.

The Bible is a book of truth, and it is inerrant. It contains no error concerning matters of our faith, morality and salvation. We read in Proverbs 30:5-6:

> *Every word of God is flawless; he is a shield to those who take refuge in him. Do not add to his words; he will rebuke you and prove you a liar.*

The Bible answers our fundamental questions about life, existence, meaning, origin and final destiny. It is God's love letter to us. The more we read the Bible, the more we hear God speaking to us. The Bible contains instructions for daily living and teaches us how God wants us to live our lives.

From reading the Word of God, we find peace and comfort. It is the food of our souls - by meditating on the Scriptures, we feed our souls. Jesus says that *Man doesn't live on bread alone but by every Word that comes from the mouth of the Lord* (Matthew 4:4).

The Bible is alive and active, and it has a transforming power. It changes us, transforms us, and renews our lives. Many people have come to repentance and new life through the power of God's Word. The Holy Spirit is present in the Word of God to bring about a change and new life in the hearts of those who listen and study it.

According to the Letter to the Hebrews 4:12:

> *The word of God is living and active, sharper than any two-edged sword, piercing to the division of soul and spirit, of joints and marrow, and discerning the thoughts and intentions of the heart.*

The Bible is also a weapon for spiritual warfare. Through it, we contradict the devil's lies (Ephesians 6:17). The Bible contains powerful stories, wisdom sayings, prophecies and narratives that give insight into who God is, who we are, and how and why we are here.

The more we read the Word of God, the more we encounter the God of the Word and the world. We also understand our faith better and are equipped to share it.

One of the effects of the Word of God is that it purifies our hearts, minds, and thoughts (Psalm 12:6; John 15:3).

The formation and structure of the Bible

The Bible is divided into the Old Testament and the New Testament. The Old Testament is the history of Israel and God's first Covenant with humanity. The Old Testament foreshadows the New Testament. The Old Testament Bible is divided into the following:

- **Pentateuch (Torah)**: *Genesis, Exodus, Leviticus, Numbers, Deuteronomy.*
  This contains the creation story, patriarchs and matriarchs, exodus and Sinai.

- **Historical books:** *Joshua, Judges, Ruth, 1 Samuel, 2 Samuel, 1 Kings, 2 Kings, 1 Chronicles, 2 Chronicles, Ezra, Nehemiah, Tobit, Judith, Esther, 1 Maccabees, 2 Maccabees.*
  This contains Jewish history, Judges and taking over of the Promised Land, kings and monarchy etc.

- **Wisdom literature:** *Job, Psalm, Proverb, Ecclesiastes, Song of Solomon, Wisdom, Sirach.*
  These are poetry, songs, witty sayings, short stories etc.

- **Prophetic books (Other divisions)**
  - Major Prophets: *Isaiah, Jeremiah, Lamentations, Baruch, Ezekiel, Daniel.*
  - Minor Prophets: *Hosea, Joel, Amos, Obadiah, Jonah, Micah, Nahum, Habakkuk, Zephaniah, Haggai, Zechariah, Malachi.*
    These books of Prophets call out for justice and fidelity to God and the covenant.

In all, there are forty-six Old Testament books in the Catholic Bible.

The New Testament is the History of Jesus and the early Church. It presents Jesus to us as the revelation of God's final plan. It is divided into the following:

- **The Gospels**: *Matthew, Mark, Luke, John.* These contain the life, ministry, teachings, and paschal mystery of Jesus.

- **Acts:** The history of the early Church.

- **Pauline letters:** *Romans, 1 Corinthians, 2 Corinthians, Galatians, Ephesians, Philippians, Colossians, 1 Thessalonians, 2 Thessalonians, 1 Timothy, 2 Timothy, Titus, Philemon.*

- **General Epistles:** *Hebrews, James, 1 Peter, 2 Peter, 1 John, 2 John, 3 John, Jude.* Note: Epistles could be further divided into Pauline, Deutero-Pauline (Paul's disciple), Pastorals (for Church leaders), and Catholic (Universal-all).

- **Revelation** – John writes apocalyptic literature during his exile in Patmos at the end of the 1st Century AD. It was written to Christians in Asia Minor undergoing extensive persecution by the Roman Empire, symbolically presenting events of the recent past as if they were occurring as part of God's final cosmic victory over evil.

Understanding the Bible

Because the Bible was written many years ago, we may be distanced from the culture and language, mode of expression and historical context of the time, and this is why sometimes we need good Catholic biblical commentaries or concordances to help us understand some of the historical, literary, and cultural contexts.

We can also understand the Word of God by listening to good teaching and sermons, and by sharing the Word of God with others, we also grow in our understanding.

We can better understand the Bible by meditating under the guidance of the Holy Spirit. This is why before we study the Bible, we need to invite the Holy Spirit to help us to understand what we are about to read.

I encourage those just starting to read the Bible to begin with the New Testament because the Old Testament contains some passages that we may not yet be equipped to understand or interpret. The Old Testament foreshadows the New Testament, and the New Testament fulfils the Old Testament and brings a clearer picture of who God is.

So, I encourage us to start with the Gospels, Acts of the Apostles, the Letters, and the Book of Revelation.

Bible study techniques

There are different study techniques I can recommend. Let me suggest two here.

I. SOAP

SOAP is a simple method for reading and applying God's Word to our lives. SOAP stands for Scripture, Observation, Application and Prayer. It involves four simple steps:

- **Scripture**:
  Read a short Bible passage aloud and write it out.
- **Observation**:
  What do you notice about the verses?
  What do you think the main message is?
  What verses, words or ideas jump out to you?
- **Application**:
  Ask God how He wants you to apply the verse to your life.
- **Prayer:**
  Pray for yourself and for others.

This method is suitable for individual and group use.

II. BIBLE
  B: **Bow** your head and pray. Pray before study, and call upon the Holy Spirit to guide you as you study the Word of God.

I: **Inspect** the Word of God. Read and gather information. Take notes.

B: **Broach** the topic. Discuss what has been read and meditate on the meaning of the Scripture.

L: **Live** it! Live meaningfully and ask God to help you apply what you have learnt.

E: **Evaluate**. At the end of the week (and the study), reconsider and re-evaluate what was learned.

Some quotes in the Bible

A well-used Bible that is falling apart usually belongs to a person who isn't. The Bible is meant to be our daily bread, not cake for special occasions. Ignorance of Scripture is ignorance of Christ.

Saint Jerome

The Old Testament is like a radio with its hidden voice announcing the One to come. The New Testament is like television because the Word became audible and visible.

Archbishop Fulton Sheen

The Bible is a love letter from God with your name on it.

Peter Kreeft

Beware of the Bible: It may change your life.

Unknown

The Bible will keep you from sin, or sin will keep you from the Bible.

Dwight L. Moody

Nature reveals God's mind and imagination, and Scripture reveals God's heart and will.

Peter Kreeft

Become familiar with the Bible so it can be your compass pointing out the road to follow.

Pope Benedict XVI

The more you read the Bible, the more you will love the author.

Unknown

The Holy Bible is like a mirror before our mind's eye. In it, we see our inner faces. From the Scriptures, we can learn about our spiritual deformities and beauties. And there too, we discover our progress and how far we are from perfection.

Saint Gregory the Great

When we pray, we talk to God; when we read Scripture, God talks to us.

Saint Isidore of Seville.

I now encourage you to read your Bible daily, to grow in the knowledge of God, His Son Jesus Christ, and who we are and why we are here. I encourage you to read the Bible and open yourself to the Holy Spirit, who will enable you to understand and be transformed. I encourage you to study the Bible to find truth, answers, comfort and peace, so you are equipped to overcome temptations and share the faith with others.

CHAPTER 11

The Holy Spirit and You

If you, then, who are evil, know how to give good gifts to your children, how much more will the heavenly Father give the Holy Spirit to those who ask him!"
Luke 11:13

Before ascending to heaven, Jesus promised His disciples and all of us that He would send us the Holy Spirit, a promise that He fulfilled and continues to fulfil. Jesus promised to give us the Holy Spirit to be our teacher, advocate, helper, comforter and friend, to lead us to the complete truth of God and who we are in Him.

The Holy Spirit is the third person of the Trinity. He is God the Holy Spirit. Take note: He is a person, which means He has will, mind and emotion; hence, we can relate with Him. A relationship with the Holy Spirit makes our spiritual life more meaningful, joyful, fruitful and peaceful.

St. Paul prayed in 2 Corinthians 13:14 that the grace of our Lord Jesus Christ (which enables us to do all things and become who we are in Christ), the love of God (which is the foundation of our relationship with God) and the communion of the Holy Spirit (which is what connects us to the life of the Trinity), should be with us.

Because the Holy Spirit is a person, having a relationship with Him is similar to having a relationship with others - it demands time, effort, attention, honesty, consistency, interaction, respect, nurturing and communication etc.

The Holy Spirit is the one who helps us to have a lively relationship with Jesus and to enter more deeply into the life of the Trinity.

- The Holy Spirit teaches us to pray.
- He teaches us how to worship God.
- He gives us understanding.
- The Holy Spirit gives us revelation and insight.
- The Holy Spirit comforts us when we grieve, are sad, disappointed or feel low.
- The Holy Spirit speaks to us and guides us.
- He convicts us of sins and appeals to us to repent.
- He speaks in us and through us.

The Holy Spirit also bestows gifts upon us. These are unique skills and abilities given by the Holy Spirit to the followers of Christ, to serve God for the common benefit of His people, the Church.

The Bible tells us of many charismatic gifts that the Holy Spirit produces when He comes upon us to empower us. These gifts include teaching, faith, healing, miracles, speaking in tongues and interpreting tongues, and discernment of spirits (1 Corinthians 12:4-11). Other gifts include prophecy, mercy, help, leadership and administration, service, and encouragement.

Isaiah 11:2-3 lists seven supernatural gifts of the Holy Spirit - wisdom, knowledge, understanding, counsel, fortitude, piety and fear of the Lord. We can read more about the gifts of the Spirit in the following Bible references: Ephesians 4:7-13; Isaiah 11:2-3; Romans 12:3-8 and 2 Peter 1:3.

The Holy Spirit also produces in us the character of God. The Bible calls this the fruit of the Holy Spirit. According to Galatians 5:22-23, these are love, joy, peace, patience, longanimity, kindness, goodness, faithfulness, gentleness, self-control, modesty and chastity.

The Holy Spirit is a life repairer

I always like to talk about the Holy Spirit as a life repairer. This is one of the most powerful works of the Holy Spirit. I know the concept of repair is something we are all very familiar with. Many of us are repairing our homes, gardens, offices, vehicles, etc. The essence of repair is to put things in order, to make them better, to put them in a better shape, form or look, to make them stronger and more durable, and to restore something damaged, worn or faulty to good condition.

In the same way, as we are not perfect, our lives constantly need repair. All of us are equally damaged or wounded in one way or another; the difference is only the degree. The Holy Spirit is a life-repairer.

We shall look at five ways that the Holy Spirit repairs us.

I. *He breaks addiction, no matter how severe.*
He liberates us from every bondage to an unhealthy lifestyle. He helps us to come out of these and be free again. He breaks the addiction to pornography, intake of hard drugs, abuse of alcohol, excessive smoking, masturbation, gambling etc. He transforms us and makes us whole and free again. He restores sanity and newness.

St. Paul tells us in 2 Corinthians 3:17:

> *Now the Lord is the Spirit, and where the*
> *Spirit of the Lord is, there is freedom. The*

> *Holy Spirit brings freedom to a soul op-*
> *pressed by the slavery of the body.*

II. *He heals and delivers us from our weaknesses and im-*
   perfections.

The Holy Spirit changes us. He helps us overcome bad attitudes that dent our character, which are not part of what we call a character of grace. Here, I am talking about those ways of behaving inconsistent with Christ's character and the conduct of children of the kingdom. These characteristics include anger, bad words, impatience, prejudice, cruelty, pride, lies, greed, and jealousy.

III. *He heals us emotionally and also physically.*

The Holy Spirit heals physically. He also causes healing and total recovery from inner wounds, such as past hurts, painful memories, after-effects of abuse, neglect, rejection, guilt, psychosomatic disorder, traumatic experiences and the after-effects of these. He heals from low self-esteem, anxiety, panic attacks, depression, and suicidal ideation. He makes us whole and integrally sound again.

Some of us are living testimonies of how the Holy Spirit has healed us from inner wounds and experiences of the past that were robbing our present of its joy, wonder and grace.

IV. The Holy Spirit creates a yearning for God in us.
This is called the gift of piety - a hunger for God, a delight in His presence. He makes spiritual exercises exciting; He illumines our minds to grasp spiritual concepts, realities and experiences. This experience creates a joy in us that I can't even find words to describe. He gives us joy in God. Put differently; God becomes our joy. We taste God's sweetness, and we won't be able to stop yearning for more of God.

V.   He produces divine attributes in us.
These are what are called the fruit of the Holy Spirit. I simply call them the character of God. He makes us joyful, peaceful, faithful, gentle, chaste, kind, good, patient, modest, loving and self-controlled (Galatians 5:22-23). These attributes make our lives very beautiful. No amount of makeup can match the beauty they give to the human person.

The question now is: "Where do I need repair?

Let us move this reflection further by examining how to make the Holy Spirit more active, or, put differently, how do we grow in our relationship with the Holy Spirit?

Everyone baptised and confirmed has received the Holy Spirit. He dwells in them through those sacraments. It is not enough to say I received the Holy Spirit at Baptism, and it was revived and renewed at my Confirmation. We should ask ourselves:

How active is the Holy Spirit in our lives?
How involved is He in our daily affairs?
How much do we consult Him and seek His help?

Let us be challenged to make the Holy Spirit that we have received active, to get Him involved in our daily lives, and to have an active relationship with Him.

How? I will reflect on a few ways.

A. Know more about the Holy Spirit:
The first step is knowing more about who the Holy Spirit is and what He does. Knowledge fosters relationships. How much do we know about the Holy Spirit? From today, let us seek to know more about Him through studying the Bible, listening to good/recommended talks and reading recommended books on the Holy Spirit.

Very importantly, we may know Him more by praying and asking the Holy Spirit to reveal more of Himself to us.

B. By engaging Him and inviting Him to be part of our everyday affairs.

Characteristically, the Holy Spirit won't invade our affairs if He is not invited. Let us remember from today that the Holy Spirit is our friend. He is a person and not an energy or force. He relates and wants to help us and get involved in our lives. Hence, we must learn to talk to Him, seek His help, call on Him, surrender to Him and acknowledge His presence and power. Let us allow Him to hold, inspire, teach, and direct us. The more we involve Him, the more active He becomes. The more active He becomes, the more meaningful, fruitful and full our lives become.

C. Obey Him

The Holy Spirit doesn't bypass our will; we still need to be willing to obey Him and heed His message. When we keep suppressing Him, denying, objecting and disobeying what He tells us to do, we are saying we do not need Him, thereby rejecting Him. He is not active where He is wilfully rejected, incessantly disobeyed and unheeded. When we disobey the Holy Spirit, we grieve Him (Ephesians 4:30).

D. Fellowship with other Christians.

When we gather together with other Christians who are yearning for God in an atmosphere of prayer and worship, we are in an atmosphere where we can experience more of the power of the Holy Spirit, where we can experience an impartation, where we can be empowered, where the Spirit can rest mightily on us and move dynamically in our lives.

E.   *The Holy Spirit speaks to and moves within us, mostly in silence and meditation when we are still open to God.*

To grow in our relationship with the Holy Spirit, we need attentive silence and meditation moments.

Being led by the Spirit/ Walking in the Spirit

St. Paul tells about being led by the Spirit and walking in the Spirit in Galatians 5:16-18:

> *[16] So I say, walk by the Spirit, and you will not gratify the desires of the flesh. [17] For the flesh desires what is contrary to the Spirit, and the Spirit what is contrary to the flesh. They conflict with each other so that you are not to do whatever you want. [18] But if you are led by the Spirit, you are not under the law.*

What does it mean to walk in the Spirit or to be led by the Spirit?

This simply means to open ourselves to the Holy Spirit and be receptive to His guidance, to allow the

Holy Spirit to prompt our thoughts, words and actions, and to surrender to Him to take the lead while we follow in obedience.

We are either led by the Spirit or led by the sinful flesh. Being led by the flesh makes us slaves to sinful habits. St. Paul gives us evidence of the works of a life led by the flesh. They are:

> [19]...*sexual immorality, impurity and debauchery;* [20] *idolatry and witchcraft; hatred, discord, jealousy, fits of rage, selfish ambition, dissensions, factions* [21] *and envy; drunkenness, orgies, and the like. As I did before, I warn you that those who live like this will not inherit the kingdom of God.*
>
> Galatians 5:19-21

When the Spirit leads us, we bear the opposite fruits of the works of the flesh. St. Paul also shares with us the fruit of the Spirit:

> [22] *But the fruit of the Spirit is love, joy, peace, forbearance, kindness, goodness, faithfulness,* [23] *gentleness and self-control. Against such things, there is no law.*
>
> Galatians 5:22-23

In conclusion, the Holy Spirit is a gift of the Father to us, through His Son. He is God's seal of ownership on us (Ephesians 1:13-14). He is given to us to help us in our spiritual journey. Without the Holy

Spirit, Christian life and demands are impossible, and our spiritual life will be dry, weary, tiring and burdensome.

The good news is that the Holy Spirit is accessible to us. He wants to be our friend, an active and vital part of our daily lives as we strive daily to follow Jesus.

NB: I have only said the minimum about the Holy Spirit. We can never say enough about Him. The more we read the Bible and open ourselves to Him, the more we grow in our understanding and experience of Him, and as we grow in Him, our relationship with God becomes sweeter and more delightful.

Read the following passages about the Holy Spirit and us:

- 1 Corinthians 2:6-16
- 1 Corinthians 3:16, 6:19-20
- 2 Corinthians 1:21-22,
- 2 Corinthians 5:5,
- Galatians 4:6
- Ephesians 1:13-14
- 1 John 3:24
- 1 John 4:13.
- Romans 8:9, 14-16

★★★★★

CHAPTER 12

Fellowshipping with other Christians

*Therefore encourage one another and build
up each other, as indeed you are doing.*
1 Thessalonians 5:11

Apart from attending Mass, where we listen to
the reading of the Word of God and receive
Jesus, the Bread of Life, one of the ways we grow in
the faith and our relationship with God is through
fellowshipping with other Christians.

Fellowship in Greek is '*Koinonia*,' and it means having a share in something or sharing something with
someone. Christians have a shared bond established
by our common allegiance to Christ. We can
strengthen our faith further and grow in the Lord
when we come together to pray, worship, or study
the Word of God.

Our spirituality should not just be limited to the

Mass. We must have a group of fellow Christians whom we have fellowship with, a place where the focus is on God, and everyone comes together to grow in Him and seek to deepen their relationship with Him. This was one of the characteristics of the early Church. They gathered together in house Churches to worship and listen to the Apostles' teachings.

The Bible also encourages and directs believers to fellowship together. We read in Hebrews 10:24-25:

> *24 And let us consider how we may spur one another on toward love and good deeds, 25 not giving up meeting together, as some are in the habit of doing, but encouraging one another—and all the more as you see the Day approaching.*

Whenever we gather together in fellowship, the focus must be on the following:

- Encountering Jesus through His Word.
- Worshipping the Lord together, in Spirit, in truth, and unity.
- Being open to the Holy Spirit as He speaks to us. While the early believers in Antioch were praying and fellowshipping together, the Holy Spirit spoke to them to set Paul and Barnabas aside for the mission that God wanted to give them (Acts 13:1).
- Praying for and with one another.

- Giving people the space to share their testimonies and spiritual experiences, to strengthen and encourage others, and to be strengthened and encouraged by others.
- It should also be an avenue to support one another in other practical and acceptable ways, helping to lift one another's burdens.

Just as the Bible encourages us to fellowship with other believers, it warns us against fellowshipping with the ungodly.

> *Blessed is the one who does not walk in step with the wicked or stand in the way that sinners take or sit in the company of mockers, ² but whose delight is in the law of the LORD, and meditates on his law day and night.*
>
> Psalm 1:1-2

Also, we have the same warning in Ephesians 5:11 (Berean Standard Bible):

> *Have no fellowship with the fruitless deeds of darkness but rather expose them.*

Also, read 2 Corinthians 6:16-18.
St. Paul tells us in 1 Corinthians 15:33, that bad company corrupts good character.

Challenges in fellowshipping together.

As good as it is when Christians come together, there are also challenges to be expected and prepared for. The devil is threatened when believers gather together to pray, and he is ready to do anything to destroy such an assembly. Usually, he attacks such gatherings by destroying their unity. This is when people start having conflict, malice, and misunderstanding and gradually degenerate into disharmony. The devil knows that disunity weakens the efficacy of communal prayers.

Also, he seeks to distract the focus - people start spending less time praying, worshipping, and studying the Word of God and spend more time chatting, gossiping, and organising social events and activities. They start having a break (recession) from fellowship, and before you know it, what is left are the relics of what was once powerful.

Another way the devil seeks to attack the assembly of praying Christians is to introduce sexual impurity among them. This is one of the common reasons why spiritual fire goes out, and spiritual brightness goes dim. People who started praying together gradually moved from praying to having illicit affairs with one another. In this way, the devil gains access and control in such gatherings.

We also need to guard against lukewarmness. Many people will embrace such spiritual gatherings, and they become lukewarm and backslide after a while. They lose interest and are no longer dedicated. People begin to prefer extra minutes of sleep to fellowshipping. They say yes to lunch, dinner, and unspiritual events and neglect praying with others. This is why we need a sense of discipline, priority, and re-evaluation of our interests.

Another problem I have seen in fellowship is the lack of dedicated leaders. It is often just a few people leading, sharing the Word of God, and coordinating. Many people just want to be passive, to receive but are unwilling to grow and be able to take up leadership roles. It is not enough to be a participant when Christians gather; we must grow to also be able to lead and support others.

Many people also withdraw from fellowships because there is no genuine concern for members. People feel unseen, left out and unsupported in their struggles and just withdraw themselves.

Conclusion

In conclusion, dear friends, fellowshipping with other believers is a great way to grow in our faith. In such an assembly, our prayers are strengthened because we unite with others, and our faith is strengthened by sharing and listening to others. Such fellowship creates an atmosphere of hearing from the Holy Spirit. We also receive great support, and we have a sense of belonging.

Let us, however, remember to guard against anything that can distract our focus, discourage members, and extinguish our spiritual fire. Let us always be very warm to people and welcome and encourage them to consider being part of a Christian group where they can meet, interact, and grow with other Christians.

Bible passages encouraging fellowshipping among Christians are:

- ➢ Psalm 133:1-3
- ➢ Acts 1:14
- ➢ Romans 1:12
- ➢ Ephesians 4:2-3
- ➢ Colossians 3:16
- ➢ 1 Thessalonians 5:11

★★★★★

CHAPTER 13

Regular Confession

No one who conceals transgressions will prosper, but one who confesses and forsakes them will obtain mercy.

Proverbs 28:13

Regular confession is important for anyone who wishes to grow in holiness. We must have a strong sense of sin, great sorrow for sins, and a desire to ensure that nothing comes between us and God. This is why we need to come as often as possible to the fount of mercy, where the blood of Jesus washes away our sins, where we approach as a sinner and go back pardoned, justified, and sanctified.

Confessing our sins to another human being is often difficult. Enduring what they have to say in response to our confession is sometimes uncomfortable. Yet, hearing the words, 'Through the ministry of the Church, may God give you pardon and peace, and I absolve you from your sins...' is priceless.

David L. Gray, in his book, *Cooperating with God: Life with the Cross* (March 2012), tells us that it is those things that are difficult to do and take us out of our comfort zone that are most essential for our spiritual growth. Indeed, they help us open ourselves up to God's healing and conforming grace because they are necessary.

Confession prefigures the particular judgement of everyone.

We read in Romans 14:10 and 2 Corinthians 5:10 that we must all appear before the judgement seat of Christ and receive good or evil according to what we have done in the body. When we go for Confession, we bring ourselves before the judgement seat of Christ. We accuse ourselves of everything we have done wrong, everything that the accuser could accuse us of on the last day. After this sincere and remorseful self-accusation, we obtain mercy and not punishment.

On the last day, it is a strict judgement of justice. At Confession, it is judgement with mercy. We remove the horror and terror of the final judgement by frequenting the sacrament of Reconciliation. Anyone who doesn't want to face the eternal judge with shame and fear on the last day can approach Him frequently, offloading and receiving mercy in time for what could have cost him/her an eternity of shame and punishment.

The benefits of confession

In promulgating the new rite of the sacrament of Reconciliation, following the Second Vatican Council, Blessed Pope Paul VI stressed the great value of frequent and reverent recourse to this sacrament (of Confession), even when only venial sins are in question. This practice is a constant effort to bring to perfection the grace of our Baptism.

Here I have itemised ten benefits of frequent confession.

I. The soul is cleansed/purified by the Blood of the Lamb. It erases our record of sin.

II. Grace is increased in a soul.

III. The will is strengthened against sin.

IV. Self-knowledge is increased.

V. More rapid growth in virtue takes place.

VI. We learn and grow in humility.

VII. We receive the strength to overcome bad habits and gain greater self-control.

VIII. We overcome a spirit of mediocrity, complacency, or lukewarmness.

IX.   It reconciles us to God and one another, restores us to the community, and enables us to receive Jesus more worthily in Holy Communion.

X.   It heals and restores. It restores peace, joy, and confidence by unburdening us and breaking the yoke of guilt. It heals us from anger, hatred, bitterness and burdens of the heart and sets us free because the Blood of Jesus is applied to our souls at Confession.

The Place of the Holy Spirit in the Sacrament of Reconciliation

It is not enough to come to Confession and recite our sins. There must be a firm purpose of amendment - a desire and decision not to go back to sins already confessed. God is merciful, but His mercy is not to be taken for granted - His mercy is on those who fear Him from age to age.

How can we persevere in our resolution not to sin anymore, or at least in our decision not to repeat the same sins?

We need the power of the Holy Spirit. We need the grace of God through the Holy Spirit. The Holy Spirit gives us strength to overcome evil habits. He transforms our desires, ambitions, appetite, interest, and hunger. The Holy Spirit creates a new hunger and a repulsion for sins that once attracted us.

Each time we come for Confession, let us ask the Holy Spirit for the following:

I. To lead us into ourselves and help us see what God is showing us. To lead us to see everything that is wrong with us and where God wants us to make amends. The Holy Spirit undertakes *spiritual scanning* for us, bringing to the fore everything we need to address, fix, reject, and repent.

II. For the grace of true conversion and trans-formation, our Confession won't just be a recitation of sins, a ritual, a liturgical routine, or a psychological relief but an intentional turning from sin and a turning towards God.

Objections to Confession

One might say: "I confess only to God." Yes, you can say to God, "Forgive me", and say your sins, but our sins are also committed against the brethren and the Church. That is why it is necessary to ask pardon of the Church and the brethren, in the person of the priest.

"But Father, I am ashamed …" Shame is also good - it is healthy to feel a little shame because being ashamed of something we have done wrong is salutary. It is terrible when a person feels no shame after doing what is wrong. Shame makes us more humble, and the priest receives our confession with love and tenderness and forgives us on God's behalf. Also, from a human point of view, it is good to unburden oneself, it is good to talk to the priest about those things weighing so heavily on our hearts.

In the General audience of the Holy Father on 19th February 2014, Pope Francis told us:

> "Do not be afraid of Confession! When one is in line to go to Confession, one feels all these things, even shame, but when one finishes Confession, one leaves free, grand, beautiful, forgiven, candid, and happy. This is the beauty of Confession!"

Things to avoid when making a confession

- Anger or provocation before or after Confession. This only shows that the penitent doesn't understand what he /she has come for.
- Confession without contrition - three conditions are necessary for making a good confession - contrition, confession and satisfaction.
- Confessing the sins of another person or reporting them or mentioning accomplices.

- Concealing sins (Proverbs 28:13).
- Justifying sins and giving excuses.
- Storytelling or converting Confession into an extensive counselling session instead of getting straight to the point.
- Vague and imprecise confession, confessing evasively and making light of the sin committed through idioms and euphemisms.
- Pretending that we can't communicate well in the language the priest can understand or deliberately subduing our voice so that the priest doesn't hear us. This, again, doesn't indicate contrition.
- Delaying penance or doing it improperly.
- Not listening or paying attention to the counsel of the confessor.

Making a Good Confession.

The basic requirement for a good confession is to return to God, just like the "prodigal son" and acknowledge our sins with true sorrow before the priest. Remember, if you need help, especially if you have been away for some time, simply ask the priest, who will help you by "walking" you through the steps to make a good confession.

Before Confession

Be truly sorry for your sins. The essential act of Penance, on the penitent's part, is contrition - a clear and decisive rejection of the sin committed, together with a resolution not to commit it again, out of one having a love for God. The resolution to avoid committing these sins or occasions of them in the future (behavioural amendment) is a sign that your sorrow is genuine and authentic. God's grace and our firm intention to rectify our life will give us the strength to resist and overcome temptation in the future.

Examination of Conscience

Before going to Confession, we should review mortal and venial sins committed since our last sacramental Confession, and we should express sorrow for our sins and a firm resolution not to sin again.

A helpful pattern for the examination of conscience is to review the Commandments of God and the Precepts of the Church:

- Have God and the pursuit of holiness in Christ been my life's goal?
  Have I denied my faith?
  Have I placed my trust in false teachings or substitutes for God?
  Have I put my faith at risk?
  Do I allow other people or pursuits to compete with God for attention, affection, and devotion in my life?

- Have I avoided the profane use of God's name in my speech?

- Have I broken a solemn vow or promise?

- Have I honoured every Sunday by avoiding unnecessary work and celebrating the Mass (and also on Holy Days)?
  Was I inattentive at or unnecessarily late for Mass, or did I leave early unnecessarily?
  Have I neglected my prayer, rushed through it, or delayed it unnecessarily?

- Have I shown Christlike respect to parents, spouse, family members and legitimate authorities?
  Have I been attentive to the religious education and formation of my children?

- Have I cared for my bodily health and safety and that of others?
  Have I abused drugs or alcohol?
  Have I supported or assisted in any way abortion, "mercy killing", or suicide?

- Was I impatient, angry, envious, proud, jealous, revengeful, or lazy?
  Have I forgiven others?

- Have I been just in my responsibilities to my employer and employees?

- Have I discriminated against others because of race or other reasons?

- Have I been chaste in thought and word?
  Have I used sex only within marriage whilst being open to procreating life?
  Have I given myself sexual gratification?
  Did I deliberately look at impure TV, pictures, and reading?

- Have I stolen anything from another, my employer, or the government?
  If so, am I ready to repay it?
  Did I fulfil my contracts?
  Did I rashly gamble, depriving my family of necessities?

- Have I spoken ill of any other person?

- Have I always told the truth?
  Have I kept secrets and confidences?

- Have I permitted sexual thoughts about someone to whom I am not married?

- Have I desired what belongs to other people?
  Have I wished ill on another?

- Have I been faithful to sacramental living (Holy Communion and Penance)?

- Have I helped make my parish community stronger and holier? Have I contributed to the support of the Church?

- Have I done penance by abstaining and fasting on obligatory days?
  Have I fasted before receiving communion?

- Have I been mindful of the poor?

- Do I accept God's will for me?

After Confession

After Confession, give thanks to God for forgiving you again. If you recall some serious sin you forgot to tell, rest assured that it has been forgiven with the others, but you may want to confess it in your next Confession.

Always remember to do your assigned Penance. If possible, do it immediately and resolve to return to the Sacrament of Reconciliation often.

We Catholics are fortunate to have the Sacrament of Reconciliation. It is the ordinary way for us to have our sins forgiven. This sacrament is a powerful help to eliminate our weaknesses, grow in holiness, and lead a balanced and virtuous life.

An Act of Contrition

Oh my God, I am heartily sorry for having offended you, and I detest all my sins because I dread the loss of heaven and the pains of hell. Most of all, I have offended you, my God, who are all good and deserving of all my love. With the help of your grace, I firmly resolve to confess my sins, do penance, and amend my life. Amen.

Quotes on the Sacrament of Reconciliation

"In failing to confess, Lord, I would only hide You from myself, not myself from You. Each one must confess his sin so that God's forgiveness, already granted on the Cross, may affect his heart and life."

St. Augustine

St. Augustine writes further:

"God accuses your sins, and if you also accuse them, you are united to God…. When your deeds displease you, your good works begin from that time, as you find fault with your evil works. The confession of evil works is the beginning of good works."

(ibid., 13: PL 35, 1191).

"Sometimes men and women prefer the darkness to the light because they are attached to their sins. Nevertheless, it is only by opening oneself to the light and only by sincerely confessing one's sins to God that one finds true peace and true joy. It is therefore important to receive the Sacrament of

Penance regularly, especially during Lent, to receive the Lord's forgiveness and to intensify our conversion process."

Pope Benedict
Angelus Address, 18 March 2012

"Daughter, when you go to confession, to this fountain of My mercy, the Blood and Water which came forth from My Heart always flows down upon your soul and ennobles it. Every time you go to confession, immerse yourself in My mercy, with great trust, so that I may pour the bounty of My grace upon your soul. When you approach the confessional, know this, that I Myself am waiting there for you. I am only hidden by the priest, but I myself act in your soul. Here the misery of the soul meets the God of mercy. Tell souls that from this fount of mercy, souls draw graces solely with the vessel of trust. If their trust is great, there is no limit to My generosity. The torrents of grace inundate humble souls. The proud always remain in poverty and misery because My grace turns away from them to humble souls."

St. Faustina
Divine Mercy in My Soul

★★★★★

CHAPTER 14

On Spiritual Direction

"While I was on my way and approaching Damascus, about noon a great light from heaven suddenly shone about me. 7 I fell to the ground and heard a voice saying to me, 'Saul, Saul, why are you persecuting me?' 8 I answered, 'Who are you, Lord?' Then he said to me, 'I am Jesus of Nazareth[a] whom you are persecuting.' 9 Now those who were with me saw the light but did not hear the voice of the one who was speaking to me. 10 I asked, 'What am I to do, Lord?' The Lord said to me, 'Get up and go to Damascus; there you will be told everything that has been assigned to you to do.' 11 Since I could not see because of the brightness of that light, those who were with me took my hand and led me to Damascus.

12 "A certain Ananias, who was a devout man according to the law and well spoken of by all the Jews living there, 13 came to me, and standing beside me, he said,

'Brother Saul, regain your sight!' In that very hour I regained my sight and saw him. 14 Then he said, 'The God of our ancestors has chosen you to know his will, to see the Righteous One, and to hear his own voice, 15 for you will be his witness to all the world of what you have seen and heard.

Acts 22:6-15

O ne of the ways that we can deepen our relationship with God is through periodic spiritual direction. Spiritual direction is a form of guidance in an atmosphere of prayer and holy conversation, that helps individuals deepen their relationship with God. It is an intentional time to sit with someone who is a companion on our spiritual journey.

These keywords are important in spiritual direction:

- Empathetic listening
- Guidance
- Prayers

The vision of spiritual direction is to help an individual to sense God's presence and actions in their lives and discern new ways to experience God and grow deeper in spirituality. Spiritual direction is different from counselling or coaching. Counselling focuses on overcoming a hurt, conflict or mental health problem. Coaching focuses on achieving goals and being more effective in work or life. Spiritual direction, on the other hand, helps us to sense and respond to God's presence amid life's challenges. It focuses on discerning the Lord's purpose in our lives.

Benefits of spiritual direction

- It helps to increase our self-awareness: a spiritual director is like a mirror through whom we see ourselves.
- Spiritual direction also provides a healthy space for us to share our experiences and to experience healing and freedom.
- It provides an intentional, non-judgemental space to reflect upon our life journey and helps us to open up to God's transforming love and grace.
- It provides a prayerful space to lament, celebrate and explore where we have come from and where we are going.
- Spiritual direction is a great cure for spiritual dryness. It is a great help when we start feeling that God is remote and we are disconnected. It helps us to sense the movement of

the Holy Spirit again and follow His prompting.

- Spiritual direction helps us to gain clarity, discern God's will when we are confused, and gain freedom of spirit.
- It gives us the atmosphere to listen to God.

Choosing a spiritual director

Let us begin by explaining who a spiritual director is, and then we can look at some things to consider in choosing a spiritual director.

A spiritual director is called to a ministry of listening, observing and guiding someone who intends to grow in their intimacy with God. Because of the importance of this ministry, one needs someone who is seasoned in spiritual matters and takes their relationship with God seriously.

Spiritual direction also takes some time. Many people have spiritual direction once a month, whilst others have it more frequently, depending on need and availability. Hence, one needs a spiritual director who is accessible and willing to listen and journey with us. Some people are knowledgeable in spiritual matters but are not available. They are too busy to commit to supporting others on their journey. Hence, it is not enough to choose someone very spiritual - we need someone who can commit to this.

We also need to pray and ask God for discernment so that God will lead us to someone who will support us. There are people we are certain would be the best for us, but that may not be the case.

Remember 1 Samuel 16:7 (New King James Version):

> *But the LORD told Samuel, "Do not look at his appearance or physical stature because I have refused him. For the LORD does not see as man sees; for man looks at the outward appearance, but the LORD looks at the heart.*

A spiritual director doesn't have to be clergy or religious. Some members of the laity are also very good and are trained in spiritual direction and in supporting others. In most cases, they are even more available, experienced and dedicated than many ordained ministers.

It would be very helpful if the person to direct others has undergone spiritual direction and safeguarding training.

Things to note

Prayer should always be the starting point of spiritual direction, and every conversation must be in an atmosphere of openness to the Holy Spirit.

Spiritual direction is a time of holy conversation, so we must not be distracted from this. Our conversation must not become mundane or essentially carnal. As much as possible, in spiritual direction, we should avoid loose talk, careless jokes, gossip, flirtatious words or actions, suggestive gestures, appearance or disposition.

If we feel a spiritual director is no longer helping us, or we are beginning to feel uncomfortable or unsafe around them, please immediately terminate the agreement. Let us not give the devil his opportunity (Ephesians 4:27).

Any intimacy and delicate friendship must be avoided between the director and the person seeking direction. Discipline is key, and the focus should always be on God. It is a grave sin when people move from spiritual direction to having illicit affairs.

Take note - a spiritual director is human. He/she is not perfect. He/she is not Jesus - as much as they are ambassadors of Jesus, they are still human and fallible. They can make mistakes, misjudge and be tempted, just like anyone else. Let us not judge or condemn them when they make mistakes but be patient and support them with our prayers, so that

God may strengthen them, speak to us through them and give them the wisdom to direct us.

However, our focus must always be on Jesus, the author and finisher of our faith (Hebrews 12:2). Only Jesus is the perfect role model for all of us. The scandal of a spiritual director must not lead to the death of our faith.

★★★★★

CHAPTER 15

Going on Retreat and the Beauty of Silent time with God

*He said to them, "Come away to a de-
serted place all by yourselves and rest a
while." For many were coming and going,
and they had no leisure even to eat.*
Mark 6:31

One of the means available for us to continue
growing and enriching our spiritual lives are
regular retreats. Retreat simply means to withdraw
or drawback. In context, a retreat is when one,
whether alone or with others, consciously sets time
aside for ourselves and for God, to rest and reflect
on our life and relationship with God.

It is a deliberate act of stepping aside from our nor-
mal routine by withdrawing (not running away)
from the noise and pressures of our daily lives to be
attentive to God and ourselves. We all need to
sometimes, temporarily leave the immediate and
demanding claims of our social, domestic, and work

responsibilities, to be in a quiet place where we are open and ready to listen to God.

Working hard without stopping doesn't help us - we burn out, we can lose touch with God, we give without getting refilled, we have no time to reflect and review, and we may even start to drift without knowing, until we end up drowning.

Jesus encouraged His disciples to always find some lonely place and rest. In Mark 6:31-32, when the disciples returned from the mission on which He had sent them, Jesus told them:

> *'Come away to a deserted place all by yourselves and rest a while.' For many were coming and going, and they had no leisure even to eat. ³² And they went away in the boat to a deserted place by them-selves.*

Why do we need to retreat?

- It allows us to just be still, step aside from everyday responsibilities, and find peace.

- It allows us to review our lives and to reflect in a spiritual environment. We are able to re-flect on who we have been, who we are, and who God desires us to be in the future. This gives us the opportunity to make amends and possibly approach God in the sacrament of Reconciliation.

- It enables us to hear from God and gain clarity about matters. When we have quiet time, we can listen to God without distraction. Listening to God gives clarity and direction.

- A retreat enables us to rest and unwind. It is good not only for our spiritual health but also for our mental and emotional wellbeing. It is a practical self-care. We are able to break away from work and family and just breathe. This will prevent us from burning out.

- A retreat provides us with a space to heal and be restored.

- During a retreat, especially with other Christians, we can build good relationships with people with whom we share a common faith and love of Jesus.

- A retreat gives us a unique opportunity to pray more, to spend time with God and to pray for others as well.

- A retreat gives us ample opportunity to experience the beauty and power of silence. It is so difficult today to just be still and get away from the noise and activities that are part and parcel of our world. We need silence and solitude to grow spiritually and nurture our souls. We must all learn to disconnect from the relentless flow of words, sounds, and the torrents of thoughts and images that are constantly bombarding our minds, day and night.

In silence we find inner peace, we discover God, just as Elijah discovered Him in the silence of a gentle breeze (1 Kings 19:10-13). We need this encounter for spiritual transformation.

Dear friends, I hereby recommend that we always set time aside for a periodic retreat, away from our regular environment. We have so many retreat centres, especially here in England, places where the beauty of nature can lead us to appreciate the God of nature and to experience serenity.

We may choose to have an individual retreat or a communal retreat (with others). Depending on what we need, it may be directed by a spiritual director or even self-directed. Most importantly, we can be in touch with God and ourselves.

Retreats refresh, revitalise, rekindle, and renew. We are able to see with new eyes, think with new minds, feel with renewed hearts, and work with new zeal so that when returning to our present re-alities after the retreat, we can go back with fresh energy, a new sense of purpose, vision and mission.

CHAPTER 16

Witnessing To the Faith

That which we have seen and heard we also proclaim to you, so that you too may have fellowship with us; indeed our fellowship is with the Father and his Son Jesus Christ.

1 John 1:3

I still remember how, when I lived in Nigeria, the Jehovah's Witnesses came to people's homes to talk about God and stood on the streets and street corners to share pamphlets and booklets with people. As a child, I listened to them and learned many biblical stories from the book that they call "My Book", which is a collection of mostly Old Testament stories. Even calling the book's name evokes memories of childhood - I can still smell the book and vividly remember the pictures in them.

Fast forward to now, and whenever I think of evangelisation, I think of what I saw the Jehovah's Witnesses do. However, evangelisation is more than that. Evangelisation, or witnessing to the faith, is a duty and privilege that all Christians have.

In legal terms, a witness is someone who testifies on behalf of a person or to an event that they have seen with their own eyes or of which they have first-hand knowledge
(This is from an article titled "What does it mean to be a witness" by Bishop Frank Caggiano, published on July 24, 2018, on the website of the diocese of Bridgeport, www.bridgeportdiocese.org).

In the Christian context, a witness testifies to their faith and demonstrates through words, actions and attitude to the sacred mystery, what they have seen, heard and believe in their heart about the Lord who has forgiven us and offered us eternal life.

So, in a nutshell, witnessing is sharing our beliefs with others but more deeply, sharing our experience of God, what He has done for us, the joy of our relationship with Him, how He has saved us, and also sharing our hope in Him.

Why must I witness?

Often, people tell themselves or believe it when others say that faith is personal and should not be talked about or that no one should try to convince others to accept their beliefs. This attitude and response have discouraged so many people from witnessing to the faith. Many people also refrain from witnessing because they don't want to be mocked, questioned, or judged. Many are shy, unconvinced, or not passionate about their faith, and some feel they are not theologically equipped and do not have enough theological or doctrinal training to witness.

Let me begin by addressing why we should witness and then talk about how we are called to witness to the Lord. I shall begin by stating why we should witness to the Lord.

I. *We are commanded to do so.*
Before Ascension, Jesus gave this as a command to the disciples. We read this in Matthew 28:19-20, where Jesus says:

> *Go therefore and make disciples of all nations, baptising them in the name of the Father and of the Son and of the Holy Spirit, [20] teaching them to observe all that I have commanded you; and lo, I am with you always, to the close of the age."*
>   See also Mark 16:15.

So, this is a mandate that all of us who are disciples of Jesus have received. This is why Jesus came first - to seek and save the lost. This is also the mission of the Church, and we share in this through our Baptism. St. Paul says, *Woe to me if I do not preach the Gospel* (1 Corinthians 9:16).

II. We must witness to the Lord because we are all branches of the vine, and we must be fruit-bearing branches (John 15:5).

We are all called to be fruitful, and the greatest fruit we can bear is the fruit of leading souls to Jesus (John 15:16).

III. We must witness to the Lord because all humans have a desperate spiritual need for Jesus.

We owe a debt to everyone around us who does not know the Lord or value their relationship with Him, especially those amongst our relatives, friends, co-workers, neighbours, etc.

St. Paul tells us in Romans 1:14:

> *I am obligated both to Greeks and to bar-barians, both to the wise and to the foolish,*

Also, in Romans 10:14, he says:

> *How can they call on the one they have not believed in? And how can they believe in the one whom they have not heard? And how can they hear without someone preaching to them?*

*IV. When we witness to the Lord, we depopulate the king-
    dom of darkness.*

The devil has held some people captive through ignorance. Knowing our Lord Jesus brings people to
freedom because Jesus delivers us from the domin-
ion of darkness and brings us to His kingdom of
light, where He makes us a chosen race, a holy na-
tion, a royal priesthood, a people set aside for the
praise and glory of God (Colossians 1:13; 1 Peter
2:9).

Anyone who brings a soul to faith has rescued that
soul from the kingdom of darkness governed by the
devil and brought them into the kingdom of light.
We read in Acts 26:17-18:

> *...I am sending you to them* [18] *to open their
> eyes and turn them from darkness to light,
> and from the power of Satan to God, so
> that they may receive forgiveness of sins
> and a place among those sanctified by faith
> in me.*

*V. We must witness to Jesus because He is the Way, the
    Truth, and the Life.*

Jesus is the way to salvation; He is the One who
saves people from eternal death. He is the way to
eternal life; He is the One sent by God so that everyone may have eternal life. So why would we not

passionately tell people how they can avoid eternal misery and enjoy eternal life?

How do we witness?

As I said, witnessing is about letting others know about the Lord. We are not called to judge or condemn people. We are not called to show that we are holier than them. We are not sent to call attention to ourselves. We are called to appeal to people to come to the Lord and experience new life in Him and, ultimately, salvation.

We are called to share with people the benefits of coming to Christ, which include:

- They become adopted children of God
- They will receive forgiveness for their sins.
- They will experience God's power to transform their lives, free them, and make them whole.
- They will experience true freedom, joy, peace and the love of God.
- They will begin to follow God's direction and purpose, fulfilling their existence's essence.

So on how we witness, I will state some practical ways we can witness to the Lord.

1. We witness by praying with zeal, faith and patience for people we know and those we encounter, and for people dear to us, that they may know the Lord and come to salvation.

2. We witness by speaking of our experience of the Lord. We don't really need much theological training to witness. After the deliverance of the man possessed by demons in Mark 5, Jesus simply told him to go to his people and tell them what God had done for him. What is most important about witnessing is telling what the Lord has done for us. We can use means such as social media to share our faith and the beauty of our faith through songs, writing, poems, customised shirts, videos, etc.

3. We witness to Jesus mostly by the example of a transformed life. When people see what God has done in us, our lives become our testimony.

4. We witness to Jesus by trying to conform our lives to the Word of God. This is about living out the Gospel values, such as charity, kindness, forgiveness, patience, truthfulness, generosity, chastity, detachment, simplicity, peacefulness and humility; in short, by the fruit of the Holy Spirit, we bear. This is how we demonstrate that we are the light of the world and give legitimacy to our message.

5. We witness to our faith by refusing to join the majority in what is wrong and standing against injustice, moral decadence, and values contradicting our Christian conscience. This is how we show that we are the salt of the earth.

6. We witness to our faith by not being afraid or ashamed to practice it, even amongst those who do not believe. For instance, we witness by praying on a bus, in the classroom, before we resume work, saying grace before and after meals, even in a restaurant, by reading our Scriptures and making the Sign of the Cross, not to show off but because that is who we are.

Let me end by reiterating that to witness effectively; we need these two things:

- An encounter: we must first encounter the Lord. A true encounter makes us passionate.
- We need the Holy Spirit to empower us to witness to the Lord. We need the help of the Holy Spirit - He is the One who directs us on how and where to witness. He gives us the words and wisdom for witnessing. He transforms our lives daily and makes us bold and courageous in witnessing to the Lord (Acts 1:8).

★★★★★

CHAPTER 17

The Call to Participate in Building the Church, the Body of Christ

7 But each of us was given grace according to the measure of Christ's gift. 8 Therefore, it is said, "When he ascended on high, he made captivity itself a captive; he gave gifts to his people." 9 (When it says, "He ascended," what does it mean but that he had also descended into the lower parts of the earth? 10 He who descended is the same one who ascended far above all the heavens so that he might fill all things.) 11 He himself granted that some are apostles, prophets, evangelists, pastors and teachers 12 to equip the saints for the work of ministry, for building up the body of Christ, 13 until all of us come to the unity of the faith and the knowledge of the Son of God, to maturity, to the measure of the full stature of Christ. 14 We must no longer be children, tossed to and fro and blown about by every wind of doctrine by people's trickery, by their craftiness in deceitful scheming; 15 but

*speaking the truth in love, we must grow
up in every way into him who is the head,
into Christ, [16] from whom the whole body,
joined and knit together by every ligament
with which it is equipped, as each part is
working properly, promotes the body's
growth in building itself up in love.*

Ephesians 4:7-16

Baptism makes us a member of the family of God's people. Through this sacrament, we become related to every Christian (Galatians 3:26-29), we become a member of the Body, we share in the mission of the Church, and we have a responsibility to build up the Church, which is the Body of Christ.

I would like to make some crucial points about the Church and our responsibilities as members.

As members of the Church, we must strive to live godly lives. However, this is not enough; we are also called to build up the Church.

The Church is there to sanctify its members, but as members, we also have a role to play to ensure that the Church remains a place where people can come and be sanctified. It means that just as we are ministered to in the Church, we must also minister to others.

We have a mandate to participate in the life of the Church and ensure that the Church, which is the Body of Christ, is healthy and strengthened.

The health and strength of the Church is not in its structure, the size of its facility, the average attendance, its programmes, its revenue or annual budget, its social media presence and followers, its sophisticated gadgets, or the organisation of its music ministry. The health, fruitfulness, and vitality of a Church are measured by the extent to which God's Word is accurately proclaimed and revered, by the presence and movement of the Spirit in the community, by the extent to which people encounter Christ and their lives are transformed, by the manifestation of the grace and power of the Holy Spirit, by the growth in the faith of the members, their hunger for God, their desire to promote unity and their passion for evangelisation.

As members of the Church, we must seek ways to help build a healthy Church and ensure that our Church is fulfilling its essence and mandate. The questions every one of us should always ask are:

What can I do in the Church?
In what ways is God calling me to serve in parish life?
What gifts have I been given, and how can I exercise them in the Church?

More practically, we need to be interested in knowing what we can do to ensure the spread of the Word of God, what we can do to draw more people to the Church and ultimately to Christ, what we can do to help people feel loved, welcomed and appreciated in the Church, to build a community spirit.

As members of the Church, we should be asking:

How can I work for the unity of members of the Church?
How can I contribute to the beauty of the Church's liturgical life?
How can I build others up in the faith?

Not everyone in the Church is called to be a leader, a priest, a deacon, Reverend Sister, or a catechist, but all of us have a role to play in the Church. We all have talents and skills, gifts and callings, and are all called to be involved in one way or another.
There are many ministries in the Church that one can think of joining. These include parish intercessors, welfare ministry, youth or children coordina-

tors, music ministry, altar servers, readers, catechists preparing people for the Sacraments, and Extraordinary Ministers of the Eucharist, especially those who take communion to the sick and homebound. We can also use our knowledge of technology to help the Church reach out to more people, or we can support the financial committee of the parish. We can help to welcome people at Mass or join those who clean the Church, etc.

There is, and there will always be, a place in the Lord for those endowed with gifts of the Spirit, such as prophecy, leadership, teaching, serving, exhortation, giving, healing, etc., as long as these are from the Holy Spirit and are humbly and wisely put to use in a way that builds the Body of Christ.

Let us remember that the overall essence of ministry is the salvation of souls, that is to lead people to Jesus by reaching the lost and perfecting those who belong to the fold.

Dear friends, the Church is a growing organism, and we all have a part to play. Let us ask the Holy Spirit to help us figure out our roles in the Church and be committed to actively contributing fruitfully to the growth of the Body of Christ.

When Jesus calls us, may we be able to answer: "Here I am, Lord, working joyfully and fruitfully for you in your Church."

★★★★★

CHAPTER 18

Take Mary as Your Mother

*When Jesus saw his Mother and the dis-
ciple he loved standing nearby, he said to
her, "Woman, here is your son," and to
the disciple, "Here is your mother." From
that time on, this disciple took her into his
home.*

John 19:26-27

To have a relationship with Jesus that excludes
His Mother is imperfect, just as it is not right
to have a relationship with a child while neglecting,
disrespecting or despising their mother. God has
given Mary to all of us, His children, so that she can
be a mother and role model to us.

According to the Gospel account of St. John, 19:26-
27, as Jesus was dying on the cross, He gave Mary
to John and John to Mary. He said, *Mother, behold
your son*, and to John, He said, *Son, behold your mother.*
The Bible says, *From that hour, John took her to his own
home* (John 19:27). John represents the Church; he
represents all the disciples that Jesus loves. Every

Christian, every child of God, every disciple of Jesus, every believer in the Lord, every soul redeemed by the Lord, must therefore reserve a space in his or her heart for the Blessed Mother of the Lord.

What the angel told Joseph is also a message for us. In Matthew 1:20, the angel said, *Do not be afraid to take Mary into your home...* We must never be afraid to take Mary home as our Mother and role model. Mary is to us everything a good mother is to a child. She intercedes for us, supports us in our moments of need, and presents us before her Son.

The Blessed Virgin Mary underwent suffering and great pain in carrying out her mission as the Mother of the Redeemer, so she can assist us in our moments of pain. The Blessed Virgin Mary can mediate the graces we need on our journey. This is why she is called the Mediatrix of Graces. According to the Catechism, no. 969, Mary is called "Mediatrix" because all grace comes from Christ, and Christ comes only through Mary, by the power of the Holy Spirit.

The Blessed Mother of our Lord can help us in our struggle for holiness and our effort to live good lives. She is able and willing to intercede for us in our needs. She can mediate and obtain divine healing, blessings and peace for us. Jesus performed His first miracle at the marriage feast at Cana in Galilee (John 2:1-11) at her intercession.

The Holy Church teaches us that she continues her maternal role even though she has been taken to heaven. Out of her maternal charity, she never ceases to intercede for us. Through her patronage, intercession and intervention, so many souls, who would have been condemned, have enjoyed God's grace and mercy. In this way, she brings terror and distress to the kingdom of Satan.

In the words of the Catechism of the Catholic Church:

> Taken up to heaven, she did not lay aside this saving office but continues to bring us the gifts of salvation by her manifold intercession. She cares for her son's brethren through maternal charity, who still journey on earth surrounded by dangers and difficulties until they are led into their blessed home (CCC 969, LG 62).

This explains why the devil will stop at nothing to plant hatred against her in the hearts of so many, even though God Himself expressed His honour when the Holy Angel Gabriel hailed her as full of grace, as someone who had found favour with God, as someone chosen to be the Mother of the Son of God (Luke 1: 26-33). Filled with the Holy Spirit,

Mary herself said, *Henceforth, all generations shall call me Blessed; for the Almighty has done great things for me...* (Luke 1: 48-49).

Her Apparitions

The Lord continues to send the Blessed Mother to us in several apparitions at different times, to call us to repentance, teach us, help us, inspire us, and obtain graces and blessings for us. In all her apparitions, she always points us to the Lord - His love for us and our need to repent and reciprocate this divine love. The more we draw close to her, the closer we are to Jesus; the closer we are to Jesus, the further the devil is from us (James 4:7-8).

Discerning Spirit

And so, any spirit that opposes love, devotion, admiration, and honour to the Blessed Virgin is not the Spirit of Christ. Any spirituality that does not accommodate the Blessed Mother of Jesus is incomplete, suspicious and deficient. To love Jesus is to love His Mother, and to love the Mother of the Lord, is to love the Lord.

Conclusion

In conclusion, I urge us to always be grateful to God for the gift of our Blessed Mother. With God as our

Father, Jesus as our Brother, Friend, King and Saviour and Mary as our Mother, we can never be orphaned; we are never alone, forlorn or unloved.

I encourage us to continue to have recourse to her, to pray the Rosary daily, to honour and acknowledge her in our prayers, to also spend time in her grotto and shrine, to adorn our homes and rooms with blessed pictures, images or statues of her, to sing joyfully in honour of her, to create a space in our hearts for her, just as the beloved disciple created room for her in his home, and most especially to ponder on her greatness and imitate her virtues. I commend the healthy spirituality of those who have 'specially' consecrated themselves to God through her. We can be sure that she will never leave any of her children.

I would like to end this exhortation with a prayer that I love so much, the Memorare:

REMEMBER, O most gracious Virgin Mary,
that never was it known
that anyone who fled to thy protection,
implored thy help,
or sought thy intercession was left unaided.
Inspired with this confidence,
I fly to thee, O Virgin of virgins, my Mother;
to thee do I come; before thee I stand,

sinful and sorrowful.
O Mother of the Word Incarnate,
despise not my petitions,
but hear and answer me in thy mercy.
Amen.

★★★★★

REFERENCES

⇒ ⚜ ⚜ ⇐

Catholic Church. 2000. Catechism of the Catholic Church. 2nd ed. Huntingdon, PA: Our Sunday Visitor.

Driscoll, Mark, 14 kinds of suffering in the Bible *https://realfaith.com/blog/14-kinds-of-suffering-in-the-bible/*

The Holy Bible, Revised Standard Version, Second Catholic Edition, Ignatian Press, San Francisco, 2006. New International Version (NIV)

Holy Bible, New International Version®, NIV® Copyright ©1973, 1978, 1984, 2011 by *Biblica.Inc.*

Kelli Mahoney, March 01, 2018; Why Is Christian Fellowship so Important? www.learnreligions.com *www.learnreligions.com/why-is-Christian-fellowship-important-712422*

Lynee Lee, 2007: Who you are in Christ, Christian-lifecoaching.co.uk *www.christianlifecoaching.co.uk/who-you-are-in-Christ.html*
Opus Dei, 03/01/2022; What is a Spiritual retreat? Opusdei.org

opusdei.org/en/article/what-is-a-spiritual-retreat/

Popcark, Dr Greg, September 9, 2022, What is Spiritual Direction and how can it help us? (Our Sunday Visitor), oursundayvisitor.com
www.oursundayvisitor.com/what-is-spiritual-direction-and-how-can-it-help-us/

Raise your sword. Who am I in Christ? Knowing my true identity
www.raiseyoursword.com

Richert, Scott P: June 25, 2019; 5 Types of prayers, learnreligions.com
www.learnreligions.com/the-types-of-prayer-542772

scripturecatholic.com, Sacrament of confession and forgiveness of sins

Smart Lemur, 8 reasons to go on a spiritual retreat-smartlemur.com
smartlemur.com/tips/spiritual-retreat

teamrcia.com, A simple history of Reconciliation for RCIA Catechists, June 2013

whitelilyoftrinity.com, Saints quotes on confession

★★★★★

BOOKS BY
FR. EMMANUEL OKAMI

⇒ 🪰 🪰 ⇐

He Sent Forth His Word, Series 1: Homilies for Sundays, Year A

He Sent Forth His Word, Series 2: Homilies for Sundays, Year B.

He Sent Forth His Word, Series 3: Homilies for Sundays, Year C.

He Sent Forth His Word, Series 4: Homilies for the Liturgical Seasons of Advent, Christmas, Lent and Easter.

He Sent Forth His Word, Series 5: Homilies for Feasts and Solemnities.

He Sent Forth His Word, Series 6: Homilies for Weekdays, Cycle I.

He Sent Forth His Word, Series 7: Homilies for Weekdays, Cycle II.

A Light to My Path: A Collection of Talks and Reflections.

His Voice Goes Forth: A Collection of Vocal Meditations and Nuggets.

Lord, Teach Us to Pray: Prayers for Various Occasions.

Pray Without Ceasing: Prayers for Various Occasions.

Seven Days Journey with the Lord: A Handbook for a Self-facilitated Retreat.

Praying with the Psalms.

What God has Joined Together: A Handbook for Marriage Preparation Course.

Whom Shall I Send: A Seven-day Journey with the Lord through His Word.

They Shall be Called My Children: Reflections and Prayers for Children.

When the Spirit Comes Upon You, Series 1:
A Nine-day Reflection and Prayers for the Gifts of the Holy Spirit.

When the Spirit Comes Upon You, Series 2:
A Twelve-day Reflection and Prayers for the Fruits of the Holy Spirit.

When the Spirit Comes Upon You, Series 3:
A Twelve-day Reflection and Prayers for the Manifestation of the Holy Spirit.

Become a Better Person: A Thirty-day Journey Towards Self-improvement and Character Transformation

Vessels for Special Use: Practical Counsels for Seminarians in Formation

In the Arms of Mary: Thirty-One Days with Our Blessed Mother
(Fr. Emmanuel Okami and Lisa Timms)

Only Say the Word
365 days of Reflection on the Word of God

A Lamp to My Feet :A Collection of Sacred Teachings

He Has Done It Before: A Collection of Testimonies of the Power of the Lord

Gone Before Us: A Series of Reflections on the Mystery of Death, Grief and Life After Death

The Unchanging Word: A Devotional Commentary and Meditation on the Bible

Citizens of Heaven: Reflections on the Lives and Legacies of the Saints in the Liturgical Calendars of England and Africa

Praying with the Bible

What God Has Joined Together: A Guide for Marriage Preparation

The Imperishable Seed: A Collection of One Hundred Inspiring Sermons and Teachings

★★★★★

Printed in Great Britain
by Amazon